DATE DUE

Principles of Course Design for Language Teaching

NEW DIRECTIONS IN LANGUAGE TEACHING
Editors: Howard B. Altman and Peter Strevens

This important series is for language teachers and others who:
– need to be informed about the key issues facing the language teaching
  profession today;
– want to understand the theoretical issues underlying current debates;
– wish to relate theory to classroom practice.

In this series:

Principles of Course Design for Language Teaching

Janice Yalden

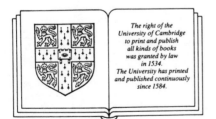

The right of the
University of Cambridge
to print and publish
all kinds of books
was granted by law
in 1534.
The University has printed
and published continuously
since 1584.

Cambridge University Press
Cambridge
New York   New Rochelle
Melbourne   Sidney

Published by the Press Syndicate of the University of Cambridge
The Pitt Building, Trumpington Street, Cambridge CB2 1RP
32 East 57th Street, New York, NY 10022, USA
10 Stamford Road, Oakleigh, Melbourne 3166, Australia

First published 1987
Second printing 1988

Printed in the United States of America

Library of Congress Cataloging-in-Publication Data
Yalden, Janice.
Principles of course design for language teaching.
(New directions in language teaching)
Bibliography: p.
Includes index.
1. Language and languages – Study and teaching.
2. Curriculum planning. I. Title.
P53.295.Y35   1987   418'.007   86–17197
ISBN 0 521 30989 1 hardcover
ISBN 0 521 31221 3 paperback

Contents

Contents

Preface

This work grows out of a dual concern for the learner and for the teacher. Because our concept of language has expanded in the last fifteen years or so to include many components other than the purely linguistic, the task of the learner has also grown. It now covers the interactional as well as the grammatical aspects of using a second language.[1] At the same time, the scope of the teacher has been enlarged, and includes enriching the teaching situation in order to allow for the changes facing the second language learner.

Although it would of course be desirable to provide sophisticated training for all second language teachers, it is obvious that not all teachers are able to obtain such training. Yet many are now expected to reorient their structure-based courses to allow for more natural language acquisition opportunities,[2] or even to plan courses that are entirely communicative or functional in nature.

This work develops an approach that permits the relatively inexperienced teacher to meet that challenge. First, the theoretical background is set out: Concepts of communicative competence and second language

1 Do language teachers teach *foreign* or *second* languages? Which do learners think they are learning? There is a long-standing distinction, especially in the United Kingdom, between foreign and second language teaching, based on the environment in which the teaching is being conducted. If the classroom language is not the language of the environment, it is a foreign language; if it is, it is a second language. However, the dividing line is not always so easily established. Although the traditional foreign/second language distinction is valid most of the time, what, for example, of students from an Arabic-speaking country learning English in Ottawa in order to enter universities in Canada? What about the children of Italian businessmen in Brussels carrying out their high school work in English? The term "foreign" implies distance – geographical originally, but psychological as well. I have preferred to use "second" throughout this work, especially since the principles of course design set out here can be followed no matter what the teaching environment may be.

2 Second language *acquisition* or *learning*? The former term has been used particularly with reference to the hypothesis that there is a natural and universal order of acquisition of morphemes independent of native-language background; more recently, Krashen (1981) introduced a distinction between "acquisition" and "learning," which he described as being different processes, the latter being conscious and available during linguistic performance only as a monitor. Krashen's distinction is referred to at more length elsewhere in this work (especially Chapter 7, and throughout Part IV). However, it should be made plain here that this distinction is not fundamental to the present work; "learning" is used in its conventional sense throughout, and subsumes "acquisition."

proficiency are examined; and speech act theory, pragmatics, and interactional analysis are discussed. Alternative solutions to the question of how to reorient language teaching in view of the new body of theory are presented critically.

In the main section of the book, a proportional approach to working out the content of a course is described. It relies on a contribution from the learner as well as from the teacher. Topics, general notions, situations, and themes provide frameworks that give support to the rest of the components to be included in a course. When frameworks are established, units can readily be produced and used in developing the kind of interactional language learning activities that a purely structural course generally cannot provide.

Procedures for developing units that could be supplementary to a structure-based course, or that could constitute the main elements of a more communicative course, are described in detail. These procedures can be applied to the preparation of courses in any language. Examples of materials developed from basic prototypes are provided, and guidance is offered on suitable classroom procedures.

The book is an introduction to contemporary views of second language course design, as well as a practical manual for the preparation of course materials. It is a blend of theory and practice. It takes readers through a series of steps intended to provide them with the skills necessary to create their own prototypical units and to transpose them into classroom-ready form. It should thus be useful both in teacher-training situations and to practicing teachers working on their own.

The projects that provided the stimulus for three sets of frameworks from which the illustrative materials in Chapters 10 and 11 are drawn grew out of a need to design courses for adult learners. The basic concepts may however be applied to the preparation of courses and materials for learners at any age or stage of second language learning.

I am very much indebted to a great many colleagues and students for discussion of the arguments on which this work is based. The time I have spent in dialogue with them has been most valuable to me, though they may not all agree by any means with the outcome of our conversations. In particular, I have appreciated discussions with Patrick Allen, Chris Brumfit, Christopher Candlin, Aviva Freedman, Ian Pringle, David Stern, and Henry Widdowson. I value greatly having worked with Maryse Bosquet, Julia Carey, George Chouchani, Alister Cumming, Brigid Fitzgerald, Joyce Pagurek, Stan Jones, and Devon Woods on the projects described in this book. I owe a debt of gratitude to all the teachers who used the experimental materials. I would also like to thank Lynne Young for her comments and encouragement at various times during the preparation of this study.

I also wish to acknowledge help and feedback from the Post Briefing Centre of the Department of External Affairs, Government of Canada, and from the language teachers there who worked with some of the materials described in this book.

I am most grateful to the New Directions in Language Teaching series editor, Peter Strevens, for his help in clarifying my ideas on a number of points, and finally, to my husband as always, for all his suggestions and his support.

Part I Usable theories

The relationship between linguistic theories and second language pedagogy is hardly a new discovery. Nor is it a matter that practicing language teachers have much time to contemplate. Nevertheless, I want to start out by suggesting that teachers who need to design their own second language courses will have a much easier time of it in the long run if they invest some effort in the study of first principles. An understanding of the prerequisites to preparing a language course includes a grasp of certain theoretical issues. Without it, the teacher may well be at a loss to understand why one suggestion rather than another is being made.

Many teachers use coursebooks that enable them to prepare and teach their lessons directly. That is, they do not need to design their own courses. However, for a variety of reasons – dissatisfaction with the concept of language teaching reflected in the single method, or new and varied needs of their students – many teachers prefer or are required to design second language courses, or at least to make modifications to existing ones. It is to the latter group that the present work is addressed.

1 Setting up a course

Setting up a new course implies a skillful blending of what is already known about language teaching and learning with the new elements that a group of learners inevitably bring to the classroom: their own needs, wants, attitudes, knowledge of the world, and so on.[1] Although there is an enormous literature on second language teaching, until recently there were few guidelines for planning out an entire course. They seemed unnecessary, since most teachers and others responsible for language courses relied heavily on textbooks containing grammatically sequenced materials. These books contained built-in sets of guidelines for the teacher: guidelines to presenting the structures of the target language and, through the drills and exercises included in the books, an implicit learning theory. By itself this seems a lot to take into account. However, when it comes to preparing to help the learner acquire the ability to use a second language in real life (and in many cases as quickly as possible), the teacher's task immediately and dramatically expands beyond the traditional limits of the structure-based course.

It expands because there have been changes in theory and practice that deeply affect the teacher's role, and because there have been equally important social changes affecting who wants to learn which language for what purpose. In what follows, I shall want to discuss both of these kinds of change and their implications for course design. I shall begin with theory and go on to more concrete matters, though the latter will keep intruding, since in language learning and teaching it is hard to remain on a purely theoretical plane for very long – the real interest lies in the classroom and in what happens there. Yet there always will remain a variety of puzzling questions about why things turn out the way they do, and what can be done to improve, modify, or rectify the situation. Hence the need for theory.

Theory and language teaching: 1

Theory in language teaching in the past has largely meant theory about the language being taught, that is to say about grammar or structure of

1 "Needs" have been defined from the learner's point of view as being arrived at externally, and "wants," internally. The term "knowledge of the world" is not used to refer to geographical knowledge, but to the sum of an individual's experience of life.

the language. For many language teachers this has been the cornerstone of their endeavors, and so when they think about choosing materials for a course, they examine textbooks with a lively interest in how the grammar and vocabulary are presented. Indeed much of the controversy in language teaching has occurred over this very issue. There is a substantial tradition of experimentation with various approaches to teaching grammar, and especially with the stock of items to be included. Further, once the items are chosen, there is the related problem of how they should be arranged – that is, how they should be graded and sequenced. Many different tacks have been taken, and many different criteria used in the process of selection and sequencing. (See, for example, Halliday, McIntosh, and Strevens 1964: 199–212; Mackey 1965: 159–226; and Smith 1971: 59–67.)

Before the introduction of scientific procedures, the writing of course materials proceeded intuitively. Much of it still does. But many very well-known coursebooks have been prepared in accordance with theoretical positions on selection, grading, and sequencing. The results of frequency studies have been widely applied. Structural analysis (which of course varies according to the theories of grammar used, and with the corpus of linguistic data being considered) has also produced many different approaches to structural language teaching. In addition, contrastive analysis of the target language and the learner's language has also formed the basis for second language coursebooks. All these approaches to preparing the target language for presentation to the learner spring from work in theoretical and descriptive linguistics. The methods produced in this way are nearly all based on a straightforward conception of the relationship between a theory of language (and possibly a theory of language learning – implicit or explicit) on the one hand, and the target language itself on the other. Figure 1.1 shows one possible representation of that relationship. (For extensive discussion of the relation of theory to language teaching see Roulet 1972; Spolsky 1978; and Stern 1983.)

Methods for language teaching

Over the years, language teachers have witnessed the elaboration of a multitude of methods, based on a variety of approaches to selection and sequencing of language items. Grammar Translation, Direct Method, the Audiolingual Method, the Audiovisual Structuro-Global Method are all well-known names in the history of language teaching. The list goes on, since successive attempts were made to pin down the essential structures and vocabulary of a language for the purpose of presenting them to its learners. The literature on second language teaching is full of accounts of these methods (e.g., Mackey 1965; Titone 1968; Kelly 1969;

4

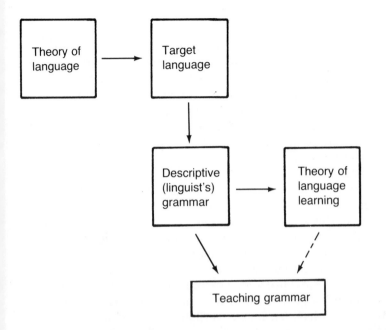

Figure 1.1 One possible model of the relationship between a theory of language and a teaching grammar.

Stern 1983; Howatt 1984). In spite of all of this activity, there has been less than total satisfaction with the results obtained, on the part of teachers as well as learners. Research carried out in the 1960s and 1970s supported these negative views of the state of language teaching based on attempts to discover and use the best method.[2] Recently, efforts have been made to reconsider the analytical model for description and comparison of methods (Richards and Rodgers 1982), and attention has been directed to the question of internal consistency of methods as well.[3] This kind of research may well throw new light on how methods may be used in course design, a matter to which I shall return at the conclusion of the present work.

2 The two classic comparative studies are Scherer and Wertheimer (1964) and Smith (1970). However, there were a great many other studies whose findings were reported in *The Modern Language Journal, Foreign Language Annals,* and other journals of applied linguistics and language teaching published in the 1960s and 1970s.
3 Michael Long, at the 1984 ABC Workshops, put forward a set of questions to be used in examining various teaching models, the answers to which he claimed would lead to further questions about the operational definition of the models or methods. See *TESOL Newsletter* 2, 1985, p. 11.

New elements in course design

More recently, attempts to apply knowledge gained from the studies of interlanguage and the procedures of error analysis have contributed yet another approach to selecting and sequencing the morphological and syntactic aspects of language. This is one in which a description of the natural processes of learning a second language is fundamental. Theoretical work on natural second language acquisition is far from complete, however, and its implications for teaching need more study. (For a discussion of the current state of second language acquisition theory and its applications, see, e.g., Lightbown 1984, 1985; and Long and Sato 1984.) Thus coursebooks based purely on interlanguage theory are far from common, if indeed any exist at all.

I shall return to this aspect of theory and practice in Part II. It is worth noting here, however, that although psycholinguistic studies of language learning have multiplied enormously in recent years, this whole area represents a relatively recent contribution to language teaching theory. It was only in the early fifties that psycholinguistics began to come together as a discipline – or as a branch of general linguistics – and only later did it begin to have an impact on language teaching theory and practice.[4] This is an area of encouraging research, however, and one that has already considerably enriched the concept of language learning and the practice of language teaching.

Theory and language teaching: 2

The method concept

The reasons for dissatisfaction with the results obtained using the model shown in Figure 1.1 (or similar models) have been discussed by Stern in his thorough treatment of language teaching theory and practice. He suggests that a break with the "method concept" has occurred, and that

> many important developments took place in the sixties and seventies which deserve our attention because they indicate a valuable new direction of thought in language pedagogy: to overcome the narrowness, rigidities, and imbalances which have resulted from conceptualizing language teaching purely or mainly through the concept of method. (Stern 1983: 477)

Methods of language teaching, together with coursebooks and other supporting materials based on them, have turned out to be unsatisfactory as *universal* solutions to problems in second language course design. Yet

4 Stern refers to Osgood and Sebeok (1954) as being "a seminal study on 'psycholinguistics' " (1983: 296). Selinker (1984: 333) states that interlanguage studies are only seventeen years old.

linguistic and psycholinguistic theory are still expected to influence approaches to language teaching. If they are to do this successfully, either the theories upon which the approaches are based will have to be changed, or *the way in which language teaching takes up the contribution from linguistic theory* will have to be altered. Indeed, quite possibly both must occur.

Applied linguistics

It is therefore not surprising that the notion of linguistic theory applied to pedagogy – or "applied linguistics"[5] – has been given a much broader interpretation in recent years than it had previously enjoyed. It includes grammatical theory, in the sense of theory of the phonological, morphological, and syntactic structures of language, and also includes learning theory; but it embraces many other aspects of psycholinguistic theory as well. Sociolinguistic theory has been a recent addition in North American work, though long of interest in Europe through the influence of the Prague School. Educational theory, particularly in the form of curriculum development, also now plays a role.

The models that are supplied to the language teacher are thus much more complex than they once were. They are attempts to account for all the sources of language teaching and to show the relationships among all of the variables involved. Although these models differ in many ways from each other, there is no doubt that they are all much more elaborate than the simple diagram shown in Figure 1.1. Teachers thus have a more difficult task ahead if they wish to understand them and to adapt their teaching to take into account the complicated structure of language pedagogy that these models represent.

Theory and the teacher

Teachers and theory: Do they really mix? Most teachers, I believe, prefer to think of themselves as practical people, engaged in busy and demanding work. And so they are – but whether they acknowledge it or not, they are constantly confronting issues on which it is necessary to take a theoretical position. Every time they choose a coursebook, every time they decide to alter the sequence in which exercises or activities are presented in a published textbook, they are taking a stand on the question of an approach to language description and presentation. When they produce their own materials, it is in response to the feeling that what is available is not enough for the needs of their class. They thus take a

5 For discussion of this term see, for example, Corder (1973), Spolsky (1978), and Kaplan (1980).

position on what those needs are – the very problems that are studied in psycholinguistics and in sociolinguistics. Often it seems that these and other problems arise in an unpredictable and disorganized way, and the road to their solution can be an extremely roundabout one. Teachers do gain immeasurably through classroom experience, of course, and beginners in the business will always do well to consult their more experienced colleagues. There are also a large number of teachers' guides and manuals available, many of which offer practical advice. Why then bother with theory?

The best answer is that theory, far from being a frill, is extremely useful, indeed indispensable. Good, usable theory not only brings the language teacher necessary knowledge but a conceptual scheme for organizing it and making sense of new ideas as they become available. It is perfectly evident now that theories developed by those who work in general and descriptive linguistics, on the one hand, and those who work in applied or educational linguistics, on the other, are not shaped in identical fashion. This is not surprising, since the goals and responsibilities of each group are different. But theories elaborated by the first group are necessary to the second, since they concern the substance with which the teacher must work: language.

There are others involved who would benefit from some more theoretical knowledge of the field as well, notably the learner and those responsible for providing the conditions under which teaching and learning will take place. But the burden generally falls upon teachers. They are visibly the professionals and the mediators between learners and the matter to be learned. The nature of the relationships among all the parties concerned is interesting, and I shall return to it. But first we need to look more closely at what teachers can expect from investing some time in gaining a deeper knowledge of theoretical problems and their possible solutions.

Using theory

It is clear that knowledge of linguistic theory by itself does not provide immediate and direct answers to practical problems. It takes both kinds of knowledge, theoretical and practical, to come up with the desired solutions. Therefore, by asking teachers to expend some effort on reading about theory before getting to the practical applications, the intention is not to subordinate one to the other. It is to ask for active consideration of various sources of knowledge, and for collaboration with linguists in asking the right questions and in getting the right answers.

There is a second point to be clarified: What is meant exactly by "theory"? This question has been of considerable interest ever since it became plain that a direct application of linguistic theories would not solve pedagogical problems. Brumfit makes the point that teaching, being "an activity which is performed, directly or indirectly, by human beings on human beings," will elicit from those who write about it more evidence of " 'personal knowledge' . . . than [from] those who write on some other aspects of human behaviour – for example, anthropologists working in a culture different from their own" (Brumfit 1984b: 5).

Both Brumfit and Stern stress that in discussing and defining the field of language teaching theory, it is important to recognize that there are various categories of theory to be sorted out. Their work goes a long way to dealing with the argument that has developed over whether and to what degree language teaching is a scientific (not a humanistic) activity. Brumfit writes about "kinds of knowledge" and "the status of various ways of knowing about something" (1984b: 5). His is a view of theory that is friendly to the teacher. In his discussion of science and of scientific procedures (which of course include the formulation of hypotheses) he writes that it is possible to "incorporate the instinct or experiential understanding of the practitioner." Who or where understanding of the phenomena being observed comes from is not important in this view, "so long as the understanding is publicly formulated and explicitly turned into testable statements." These "testable statements," furthermore, can be arrived at only through the application of understanding "in relation to specific problems to be solved" (Brumfit 1984b: 10).

Strevens (1985b) takes a somewhat different approach: He distinguishes four paradigms of language learning and teaching, which he labels *theory-dominated, learning/teaching dominated, mystique-dominated,* and *literature-dominated.* These could be arranged in a continuum, according to the degree to which they are viewed as scientific or not. The first, which Strevens calls "fundamentally a branch of theoretical linguistics," is the most scientific; the second is eclectic (used as a term of approval), "informed by wide-ranging principles and aspects of theory, but not dominated by them." The third, while consonant with some schools of thought in psychotherapy, is not scientific in the same sense as is linguistics; and the fourth, being a branch of literary studies, is "not concerned with the systematic teaching and learning of *language*" (pp. 2–3). This is a helpful approach to the question, especially as Strevens insists that none of the paradigms is better or worse than the others, but that each operates within its own universe of discourse. He is concerned mostly with the learning/teaching-dominated paradigm, as I am here. The others serve ends that are not the subject of the present study.

What is necessary in language teaching is understanding arrived at in a variety of ways including both the procedures of the scientist and the intuitive approach of the practitioner; clear specification of the problem to be solved; and tentative solutions expressed precisely enough to be testable. Finally, the assessment of the solutions needs to be carried out publicly, with every effort to ensure that claims made about the solutions are in fact true – actually a difficult but very necessary job. This is in fact a problem-solving approach, in which scientific procedures can be used, and in which theory is essential.

When Stern talks about theory in relation to language teaching, it is not about something of interest only to those who live in ivory towers. It is useful and usable; and it also builds confidence. He writes:

As a result of theorizing, the practitioner – far from feeling caught up in scholastic battles or misled by the trappings of scholarship – should gain a sense of greater professional assurance and develop a fellow feeling with practitioners in related fields. (Stern 1983: 31)

His definition of second language teaching theory allows, as does Brumfit's, for contributions from a great many sources. Since he defines it as "the thought underlying language teaching," it is implicit in all practice. He points out that theory-building for language teaching is still going on. This is an important observation, which needs to be kept very much in mind. There are so many issues that are not settled; the teacher needs to accept that they are not, but at the same time must continue to participate in the search for answers.

Stern also presents us with a useful set of categories for assessing theory and theoretical claims in second language teaching. He speaks of "theory" in three different senses. The first (T1) is "the systematic study of the thought related to a topic or activity." This is the broadest definition, theory as offering a "system of thought, a method of analysis and synthesis, or a conceptual framework in which to place different observations, phenomena, or activities." The second definition (T2) subsumes what are often referred to as language teaching methods, approaches, philosophies, or schools of thought. The third definition (T3) is the concept as employed in the natural and human sciences as "a hypothesis or set of hypotheses that have been verified by observation or experiment" (Stern 1983: 25–6). Thus, there is room in theory-building to consider all sorts of possible contributions – including, evidently, that of the teacher.

Where does this book fit in? What can the teacher get from it? It is not concerned with basic theory of language or of learning. It *is* concerned with theory at the level of approach. It is not concerned with method as it is usually defined. It *is* concerned with the establishment of principles according to which second language courses may be designed, and in particular with what principles have to do with the use of language. What the teacher is asked to consider is presented in the following three parts: Part II – some *theoretical questions* that are of particular importance in current discussions of second language teaching theory; Part III – some *problems in course design* that are a blend of theory and practice; Part IV – a *framework for course design* into which the teacher's and the learner's contributions may be inserted, and which can be modified according to the circumstances in which it is used. This is, then, a book at Stern's T2 level – a language teaching theory based on experience. It is illustrated with many applications. (These are descriptions of second language courses that have been designed using the framework, in a number of contexts and for a number of different groups of learners.) It aims to make the theory thus presented useful and accessible to teachers who may be working in all kinds of different educational contexts, and teaching any second language to learners of any age.

Part II Language teaching and linguistics: current issues

In the Preface, I stated that our concepts of language and of language learning have expanded to include many components other than the purely grammatical. This means that the learner may well be working toward proficiency in interactional (as well as transactional) use of a second language. The work of the teacher may also have to expand, so as to enrich the teaching situation accordingly. In this section, I look at how and why all of this is happening, and what it means for language teaching at the present time.

Within the traditional (that is, structure-based) course, the teacher's role was clear and unassailable. In addition to knowing the vocabulary of the target language, he had to know all about its structures (grammar and phonology), and how to carry out drills and exercises within the method being used.[1] Good teachers have always been creative people who adapted textbook materials to meet the needs of their students; many have written, drawn, and recorded their own teaching materials as well. But their basic role had not altered in any fundamental way over the years.

In the early 1970s a number of changes began to seem desirable. Some second language teaching, it was true, had produced perfectly acceptable results, given the context and the conditions for learning. Some of it, on the other hand, was not satisfactory, unsuited both to ways in which students learned and to the purposes for which they might want to learn. Changes had taken place in the 1950s and 1960s that had significant implications for language teaching, and that seemed to indicate that modifications were going to be required.

Some of these developments had taken place in the world at large, and some in the world of linguistics. Changes in the outside world brought about a different distribution of languages being taught and a different distribution of learners – and they often had goals that the teacher of earlier years would not have anticipated. Changes in linguistics meant above all the inclusion of the sociolinguistic component in linguistic theory.

1 I have used the pronouns "he/him/his" in this book as unmarked for gender, wherever stylistically appropriate. I am generally in agreement with the tendency to eliminate sexist language in academic writing; however, these pronouns can still be understood as unmarked for gender, and their use makes for greater economy of style.

In language teaching today, these changes are being recognized and dealt with. Although courses based on structures are still very widely used, other aspects of language are receiving increasing attention in the classroom. Their identification and description have important implications for teaching. Three areas of research and discussion are especially important for course design:

– the concept of proficiency in a second language
– the pragmatics of language use
– the field of discourse analysis.

These will be treated in Chapters 2, 3, and 4. Many of the concepts introduced in Chapter 2 are discussed at length in Chapters 3 and 4. Some readers may prefer therefore to look at Chapters 3 and 4 first, and then go back to Chapter 2.

2 Proficiency in a second language

In traditional approaches to language teaching, the degree of proficiency that a learner achieves is described in terms of his mastery of "structures" – that is, of the phonology, morphosyntax, and lexicon of the target language. What matters is whether or not – or to what degree – he has learned the sounds of the target language, a certain amount of grammar, and a certain number of words. Although all of the sounds have to be attempted, the number of words and amount of grammar are usually specified in advance of a course of study. The specification can vary widely from course to course. Learners also vary widely in the degree of mastery of structures that they attain.

Even so, this kind of knowledge in itself is not adequate for those learners who want to learn a second language in order to make use of it rather than to know *about* it. It is a commonplace now that languages are learned so that people can communicate with one another. And it is well known that communication involves more than structure. But what exactly constitutes proficiency in a second language? How can it be described? To appreciate revised notions of proficiency, it is necessary to look briefly at Noam Chomsky's early work and the reactions to it that came from anthropologists, philosophers – and other linguists.

Theories of competence and performance

Chomsky's distinction

Chomsky's distinction between linguistic competence and linguistic performance provided, in its original form, a powerful stimulus for new developments in linguistics. His definition of linguistic theory as mentalistic (concerned with discovering a mental reality underlying actual behavior) came as a challenge to behaviorist theories of linguistics, in which the object of study was physical verbal behavior that could be directly observed. Chomsky made a distinction between linguistic competence (what the speaker knows, what the linguist should be concerned with) and linguistic performance (what the speaker does, i.e., says or writes, at any given time, and what the linguist should *not* be concerned with). He offered the following explanation of his distinction:

Language teaching and linguistics

[The] serious discipline [of linguistics is] concerned primarily with an ideal speaker-listener, in a completely homogeneous speech-community, who knows its language perfectly and is unaffected by such grammatically irrelevant conditions as memory limitations, distractions, shifts of attention and interest, and errors (random or characteristic) in applying his knowledge of the language in actual performance. (Chomsky 1965: 3)

He considered that samples of speech and writing obtained from native speakers should not be the data on which linguists worked, since they contain errors in performance and are therefore misleading. He also wrote that a generative grammar was an attempt to "characterise . . . the knowledge of the language *that provides the basis for actual use of language* by a speaker-hearer" (my italics). He later made an even stronger claim, to the effect that linguistic competence meant that the rules of grammar were internalized in the head of the speaker, and provided the basis for the speaker's understanding of linguistic relations.

Opposing views

Chomsky had sought to limit very strictly the field of investigation of the linguist – too strictly for some others who were also involved in the study of language. The most influential reaction to Chomsky's claims, from the point of view of language education, came from Dell Hymes. He pointed out that Chomsky's category of competence did not provide for language use – but neither did his category of performance, which includes only psychological constraints on performance and ignores all aspects of social interaction. Neither category allows for characterizing the appropriateness of what we say or write to any given social context. Hymes wrote that the image Chomsky's work conjured up for him was that of "an abstract, isolated individual . . . not, except incidentally, a person in a social world" (1972: 272).

Hymes believed that a different theory of language was needed by individuals involved in language development, who were consequently at work on practical problems *as well as* theoretical ones. It would have to deal with many things that Chomsky's theory could not handle, in particular a heterogeneous speech community, differential (not standard) competence, and the constitutive role of sociocultural features (Hymes 1972: 275). In such a theory, competence would be defined differently, to include interactional competence, and it would be called "communicative competence." It would be a theory of language users and language use, and would recognize that language users make four kinds of judgments as they speak or write, not two only, as Chomsky claimed. Chomsky's theory includes judgments of grammaticality and acceptability to the native speaker. Hymes's theory of communicative competence, linking linguistic theory to a more general theory of communication and culture, involves judgments of four kinds: whether something (be it a linguistic or some other form of communication) is

– possible, given the forms of expression available
– feasible, given the means of implementation
– appropriate (adequate, happy, successful) in relation to a context
– actually performed (and what its performance entails).

A sentence (a linguistic example of communication) may therefore be grammatical, awkward, tactful, and rare – or grammatical, easily understood, insulting, and frequent – and so on.

Hymes thus refuses to accept a model that defines the organization of language as consisting only of rules for linking referential meaning with sounds used for its expression.

Such a model implies naming to be the sole use of speech, as if languages were never organized to lament, rejoice, beseech, admonish, aphorize, inveigh ... for the many varied forms of persuasion, direction, expression and symbolic play. A model of language must design it with a face toward communicative conduct and social life. (Hymes 1972: 278)

The first step in enlarging the concept of competence had been taken. Hymes had suggested that grammaticality is only one of four sectors of communicative competence, whereas for Chomsky grammaticality *was* competence. Inevitably, applied linguists and language teachers have been drawn into the debate over the communicative function of language, since it affects both preparation for teaching and the process of teaching itself. The definition of competence has become increasingly complex, as various models are proposed from the perspective of teaching and testing.

Before looking at some of these, it is probably well to recall that, in developing his theory of generative grammar, Chomsky preferred not to connect it with the manner in which language is used in communication. Nor were the implications of his theory for language teaching of very much concern to him.[1] In the context of discussion of sociolinguistic contributions to language teaching theory, the reader should remember that his theories are mentalistic and can best be appreciated as a reaction to behaviorist approaches to linguistics. Hymes, on the

1 Chomsky made a rare appearance at a conference on language teaching in 1966, at which he said, "I am, frankly, rather sceptical about the significance, for the teaching of languages, of such insights and understanding as have been attained in linguistics and psychology" (Chomsky 1966: 43). In a later interview he said with specific reference to language teaching, "My own feeling is that from our knowledge of the organism of language and of the principles that determine language structure one cannot immediately construct a teaching program. All we can suggest is that a teaching programme be designed in such a way as to give free play to those creative principles that humans bring to the process of language learning, and I presume to the learning of anything else" (Hampshire 1968).

17

other hand, was concerned with language in use; and it is equally important to note that he assumed that linguistic theory was to be integrated with theory of communication and culture.

There are, however, linguists as well as ethnographers who simply reject, rather than try to expand upon, Chomsky's definition of competence. One of these is Halliday, who is interested, as a linguist, in language in its social context, and in the way language functions are realized in speech. Linguistics, for Halliday, is concerned with the description of speech acts, because it is only when language is in use that all its functions, all components of meaning, are operating at the same time. (See Chapter 3 for a definition of "speech act" and a discussion of speech act theory.) He is therefore not persuaded that a distinction between idealized knowledge of a language and actualized use is necessary at all for the study of language in a sociological context.

The study of language in relation to the situations in which it is used – to situation types, i.e. the study of language as 'text' – is a theoretical pursuit, no less interesting and central to linguistics than psycholinguistic investigations relating the structure of language to the structure of the human brain. (Halliday 1970: 145)

Hymes and Halliday: two different ways of dealing with Chomsky's competence–performance distinction, both of which affect the concept of proficiency in language by adding to it the dimension of social appropriateness or social context. There are of course other influences on current notions of language use and of proficiency in language use,[2] but Hymes's concept of communicative competence has proved particularly useful to applied linguistics and to language teaching. It affects deeply notions of what should or can be taught and what sort of preparation and responsibility the language teacher should have. An assessment of the current status of definitions of communicative competence is thus required.

The theory in language education

Some linguists work more closely with problems in language development and language education than others. These are traditionally called "applied linguists," though it may be argued that they are simply linguists like any others. The convention is to refer to applied linguistics when discussing theory of language education, or of language teaching, and I will adhere to that usage. In any case, I want to turn to certain linguists

---

2 Extended discussion of the development of the concept of communicative competence can be found in Munby (1978), Brumfit and Johnson (1979), Canale and Swain (1980), Canale (1983), Savignon (1983), and Stern (1983).

whose work has influenced the development of the concept of communicative competence and hence of proficiency in a second language.

These linguists have felt that if language is to be studied in its social context, and if communicative uses of language are those that are of primary interest in such studies, then the features of linguistic communication need to be defined. Attempts to characterize both verbal and written communication have proliferated since the early 1970s; as far as language teaching is concerned, there have been three notable contributions. One is the work on the communicative functions of language, undertaken by a group of linguists who were brought together by the Council of Europe in Strasbourg; a second comes from studies in the analysis of discourse; and the third is a conceptual framework for applied linguistics within which the components of communicative competence may be described.

Let us return now to the issue of the relevance of theoretical work to language teaching, and the importance for course design of an expanded notion of competence. It is fortunate that a considerable amount of work has been done to make theoretical studies more accessible to language teachers. It seems evident now that, in the search for a conceptual framework, a Chomskyan orientation is not appropriate if communicative aspects of language are to be taught or learned. Chomskyan linguistics, with its theory of innate ideas, and the notion that because ideas are innate they cannot be learned but only developed without conscious effort, is not useful in language course design. Linguistic systems can and have been learned consciously, and have been taught for a very long time.

Whether this kind of grammatical knowledge can be converted into grammatical competence for a second language, and whether it alone enables the learner to communicate, are questions that have been and will continue to be examined. For the moment, I want only to emphasize that a conceptual scheme based on a sociolinguistic view of language (taking into account contextual factors as well as the psycholinguistic aspects of communication) had become a pressing need by the end of the 1970s. There have since been many theoretical statements, comprising various descriptions of the components of communicative competence. They are all characterizations of the interaction of subsets of systems of rules in verbal behavior. A discussion of some of the most interesting and influential work follows.

Components of communicative competence

Michael Canale and Merrill Swain (1980) established an important conceptual scheme within which to examine the relationship of theory to practice. Based on an extensive review of the literature, they identified

19

three subsets of systems; in a later article, Canale (1983) expanded the description to four. He writes of the nature of linguistic communication that it

(a) is a form of social interaction, and is therefore normally acquired and used in social interaction;
(b) involves a high degree of unpredictability and creativity in form and message;
(c) takes place in discourse and sociocultural contexts which provide constraints on appropriate language use and also clues as to correct interpretations of utterances;
(d) is carried out under limiting psychological and other conditions such as memory constraints, fatigue and other distractions;
(e) always has a purpose (for example, to establish social relations, to persuade, or to promise);
(f) involves authentic, as opposed to textbook-contrived language; and
(g) is judged as successful or not on the basis of actual outcomes.

(Canale 1983: 3–4)

Taking into account this concept of linguistic communication, Canale and Swain (1980) provided a specification of three interacting factors. Canale (1983) later subdivided one of these factors, listing a total of four areas of knowledge and skill:

– grammatical competence (mastery of the language code)
– sociolinguistic competence (appropriateness of utterances with respect both to meaning and form)
– discourse competence (mastery of how to combine grammatical forms and meanings to achieve unity of a spoken or written text)
– strategic competence (mastery of verbal and non-verbal communication strategies used to compensate for breakdowns in communication, and to make communication more effective).

(Canale 1983: 9–10)

In neither account is a model provided – a description of *how* these factors interact with one another – this was left to later research.

A significant key to the understanding of Canale's conceptual scheme is his treatment of the distinction between communicative competence and "actual communication," or what others call "performance." He points out that in Canale and Swain (1980) communicative competence was understood as the underlying systems of knowledge and skill required for communication. For example, to communicate one must have knowledge of vocabulary, but also skill in using the sociolinguistic conventions of a given language. A distinction was therefore drawn between the underlying systems of knowledge and what Canale labels actual communication: the realization of such knowledge and skill under limiting psychological and environmental conditions, such as memory and perceptual constraints, fatigue, nervousness (Canale 1983: 5). It is very

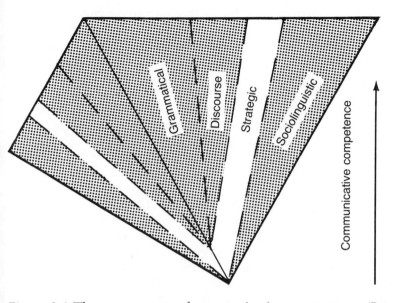

Figure 2.1 The components of communicative competence. (Based on S. Savignon, *Communicative Competence: Theory and Classroom Practice*, p. 46, © 1983 Addison-Wesley. By permission.)

important to note that in both Canale and Swain (1980) and in Canale (1983), "communicative competence" is used to refer to both knowledge *and* skill in using knowledge. Skill in communicating is not, for these researchers, a part of the theory of performance.

Sandra Savignon, who carried out one of the earliest research studies on communicative competence (1972), proposes a possible relationship among the four factors. (See also Savignon 1983 for further discussion of Canale's four components, which she accepts.) Although she makes it clear that her model is merely intended "to serve heuristically for other integrative descriptions" (Savignon 1983: 45), it takes theory another step closer to the classroom. She intends her diagram (Figure 2.1) to show that the components interact constantly; that in communication one does not go from one to the other "as one strings pearls on a necklace" (1983: 45). She also suggests that a certain sociolinguistic and strategic capacity allows the learner a measure of communicative ability, *even before the acquisition of any grammatical competence*. She suggests further that strategic competence is always present, even – or especially – at the beginning, and that it diminishes in importance as other components increase. It always remains, however, since one never knows *all* of a language – even one's own. It is important to stress again that for all of these researchers, the key to the understanding of communicative competence is its interactive nature.

Diane Larsen-Freeman provides another interesting interpretation of communicative competence. "In order to fashion our utterance and use it appropriately within a context," she writes, "we must minimally make use of our knowledge of linguistic rules, functions or speech acts, propositional content, interactional patterns, and strategic competence" (Larsen-Freeman 1982: 109). This is a somewhat different conceptual scheme from Canale and Swain (1980) or Canale (1983). Larsen-Freeman includes both discourse and paralinguistic areas in the subset of linguistic rules. Propositional content is treated as a separate subset, whereas it is included, implicitly or explicitly, in the subset of discourse by other researchers (e.g., Canale 1983). Larsen-Freeman points out that this area seems not to have been regarded as being as fecund as the area of speech acts in linguistics (although of course it has always been central in philosophy), and that accordingly, the research potential of what she regards as a separate area of communicative competence has hardly been tapped (Larsen-Freeman 1982: 115). She includes the coherence property of language in this area, whereas Canale (1983), for example, clearly sees it as part of the discourse subset.

Another of Larsen-Freeman's subsets, interactional patterns, is not treated separately in Canale and Swain (1980) or in Canale (1983). These and other researchers would include interactional patterns under discourse. However, the researchers cited all agree that strategic competence is distinct and indeed qualitatively different from the other subsets. As Larsen-Freeman puts it, it seems to entail a dynamic process: "It is a superordinate process responsible for controlling the smooth flow of communication" (1982: 118).

In still another recent examination of communicative competence, Lyle Bachman and Adrian Palmer (1982), basing their work on the Canale and Swain (1980) scheme of linguistic, sociolinguistic, and strategic components, posit three distinct traits of communicative *proficiency* (note the shift in terminology) – linguistic competence, pragmatic competence, and sociolinguistic competence. Figure 2.2 illustrates their theoretical scheme. It clearly has the status of a model, in that it does make claims regarding the interaction of the different abilities or constructs involved.

Finally, Faerch, Haastrup and Phillipson (1984: 167) state that communicative competence consists of phonology/orthography, grammar, lexis, pragmatics, discourse, communication strategies, and fluency – again a somewhat different list.

Interpretations and applications

I have described several attempts to come to terms with what language as communication means in language education. It is clear that a con-

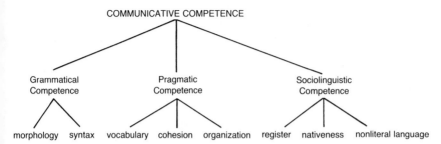

Figure 2.2 Bachman and Palmer's theoretical scheme of communicative competence. (From L. F. Bachman and A. S. Palmer, "The construct validation of some components of communicative proficiency," *TESOL Quarterly* 16/4, p. 451. © 1982 by Teachers of English to Speakers of Other Languages. Reprinted by permission.)

sensus does not yet exist on the components of communicative competence, let alone the implications of the concept for language teaching. The notion of *fluency,* included in Faerch et al. (1984) as one of the factors, has been defined by Brumfit (1984b) in contradistinction to that of *accuracy.* Brumfit states it is "essentially a methodological distinction rather than one in psychology and linguistics" (p. 52). It would appear, therefore, that in some definitions of communicative competence there is confusion – or at least overlap – among the categories of factors being considered for inclusion. Any attempt to fit all of the factors so far suggested into a grid will reveal the problem of categorization.

All of this will serve to remind that "communicative competence" is not something to be acquired like a new pair of shoes. It is a concept that has been developed in order to try to explain and predict certain phenomena. Our understanding of the nature of second language proficiency will continue to evolve, as will the model or models used to describe it. One of the most controversial aspects of the whole discussion still is whether or not grammatical competence is to be considered a part of communicative competence. Jakobovits, for example, in his specification of the aspects of knowledge that he considered part of communicative competence, omits grammatical competence (1970). If linguistic or grammatical competence is omitted, however, then the relationship between it and the other factors in a person's competence is deemphasized or rejected. This is quite inconsistent with definitions of language as communication (e.g., that of Hymes). Although Jakobovits did not draw such conclusions, they can and have been drawn.

The issue is further clouded by Krashen's work on Monitor Theory (Krashen 1981, 1982; Krashen and Terrell 1983). His distinction between "learning" and "acquisition" and the implications of his work

23

for classroom teaching have given rise to doubts about the wisdom of teaching grammar as a means of developing linguistic competence. If grammatical competence were an area that could not be developed directly through teaching, then teaching for development of the other factors in communicative competence would be the only possible alternative. The definition of language as communication, however, requires that grammatical competence be included as a component. Furthermore, recent research (e.g., Long 1983a) lends new support to the long-established view that grammatical competence can indeed be taught directly. The issue that needs attention is rather what the goals of language teaching should be, in terms of what sort of proficiency learners need to develop. (Larsen-Freeman 1982: 109–20 provides a review of the literature especially oriented toward the classroom teacher, as well as a very full bibliography. Canale and Swain 1980 and Savignon 1983 are also both excellent references for further discussion and for bibliography.)

Two concepts of proficiency

If one looks at the definition of proficiency itself, one finds that there are two separate concepts that govern contemporary approaches to teaching and testing:

1. The concept of a *standard or generalized* definition of proficiency. It entails the setting of tests by some central body, whether it be a group of teachers, an institution, or an educational authority. It assumes some uniformity in instruction, and also that input in the form of items taught ought to equal output in the form of items learned. It also means that teachers and those responsible for the preparation of curricula or syllabuses can determine the syllabus upon which testing would be based.
2. The concept of *variable definition of proficiency*. It governs an approach in which input is believed to be affected by the learner's processing before it can turn into output. Preparing a syllabus therefore becomes more complex, as there are several sets of factors (components of communicative competence) to be dealt with, and allowance must be made for variation in the goals and purposes of the learners, as well as for their personal characteristics.

The concept of the standard definition originally stemmed from a view of linguistic competence as unitary, that is, consisting only of grammatical competence. The concept is now being extended to include all the components of communicative competence – although exactly what these are is still debated. The concept of *variable definition* became important early in the development of courses in English for specific purposes (ESP). Its adoption has led to a multitude of special-purpose courses for adults, as well as General English and other courses which are more flexible than previously, and in which the syllabus and the tests are affected by a needs analysis. For the teacher, this means that the concept of a single course, a single unchanging approach to teaching, has to be abandoned, and that the issue of course design for second language teaching takes on new importance.

One can of course expect communicative competence and actual communication to vary from learner to learner, and one can expect variable objectives or goals as well. But to say that "communicative competence, as a concept, can mean different things for different groups of learners" (McGroarty 1984: 257) is to miss the point: The *concept* does not vary. The objectives of second language courses can and do.

Nor is communicative competence in its turn a component of language proficiency.[3] On the contrary, definitions of proficiency are based upon definitions of competence. If one accepts Hymes's or Halliday's definition of language as communication, for example, one necessarily accepts a definition of competence as having several components – and one's definition of proficiency will also be componential, and will include linguistic proficiency, along with a number of other factors. Savignon underscores "the tension that presently exists between the encouragement of second-language use, or functional proficiency, on the one hand, and a renewed emphasis on discrete points of sentence-level grammar, or accuracy," on the other (Savignon 1985: 130). This tension evidently springs from the differences between those who have a commitment to functional versus structural definitions of language. In language teaching, I have argued, the functional definition takes methodology and course design much further forward than does the structural.

Communicative competence as a goal

In the field of second language teaching itself, there does appear to be agreement that full communicative competence can be, but does not *have* to be, an appropriate goal at all levels, even for beginners, and that it does not have to be confined to programs for adults at an advanced level nor to extra-institutional settings. I should make it clear that I am using "communicative competence" as defined by Savignon, who gives what is to my mind the most acceptable and useful definition:

3 Politzer and McGroarty refer to "four English language proficiency measures: linguistic competence; auditory comprehension; overall oral proficiency; and communicative competence, conceptualized here primarily as the ability to convey information" (1985: 103). In this view, not only is communicative competence a *component* of proficiency, but it is very greatly reduced as a concept. In any event, it is not clear how one would convey information verbally without linguistic competence.

Functional language proficiency; the expression, interpretation, and negotiation of meaning involving interaction between two or more persons belonging to the same (or different) speech community (communities), or between one person and a written or oral text. (Savignon 1983: 303)

This definition contrasts strongly in its richness with the usual notion of grammatical competence as being knowledge of the structure of a language at the sentence level. Its adoption therefore implies a commitment to the provision of a learning environment that will provide opportunities for the "negotiation of meaning" rather than for an examination of language structures and their practice.

If this definition is accepted, one can readily appreciate work on curricula for general education undertaken to provide the kinds of opportunities referred to earlier (van Ek 1976; Gouvernement du Québec 1980). There have also been numerous reports on immersion teaching (Swain 1981; Genesee 1983), which is certainly a form of teaching for communicative competence. The immersion approach to bilingual education had its beginnings in a Montreal primary school in 1965. Very briefly put, it consists of teaching regular school subjects through the medium of a second language, so that learners become accustomed to using the second language, not as a goal in itself, but in pursuit of the goals inherent in the overall curriculum. Use of the mother tongue is phased in gradually, but begins only after a certain period of instruction in the second language is completed. In the Canadian context, the second language being thus learned is French, the learners are speakers of English, and the initial period of total immersion is usually a year. Several versions of this approach are now in practice, known as "early" or "late," "partial" as well as "total." In spite of acceptance of the wide applicability of these expanded goals, however, much exploration of the means of providing them in a wide range of educational settings is still required.

Generalized versus variable proficiency

The language teacher who has responsibility for course design and planning is still left without a final decision concerning which of these two concepts of second language proficiency to use: generalized or variable. One major problem is whether there can ever be a generalized set of guidelines for functional proficiency. If it were possible, how could generalized standards of second language proficiency be expressed, given the possibility of uneven development of some or all of the "competences" in the individual learner? So far, four responses to this question have emerged.

The first is to deny the need for guidelines, and argue that the actual learning outcomes in any given teaching situation can be the only description of proficiency possible. (Stern 1983: 341 makes a distinction between proficiency seen as a goal and proficiency seen as a fact, which would probably dispose of this argument.)

The second is to specify the anticipated outcome for learners or groups of learners who want a second language for a specific purpose (e.g., Munby 1978; B. Carroll 1980).

The third is to attempt to produce generalized proficiency guidelines that would be applicable to all learners (e.g., the Foreign Service Institute ratings, and the ACTFL Guidelines, which are inspired by the FSI ratings [James 1985]). This solution nevertheless entails stringent structural requirements (see Savignon 1985 for discussion).

The fourth is the response provided by the present work, in which generalized frameworks for teaching and learning are used to produce a variety of second language courses. The learner's contribution to such frameworks can lead to a high degree of individualization of objectives, instruction, and learning outcome.

Whatever the merits of these interpretations may be, generalized guidelines are unsatisfactory in many situations. Thus, if the concept of variable proficiency is accepted, a complex definition, or series of definitions, of proficiency have to be worked out, with a corresponding effect on methodology and classroom techniques. This is the reason for the introduction of the discussion of proficiency here; the means whereby one may work from a concept of proficiency to the design of a particular course is described in Part IV.

3 Language functions and pragmatics

I suggest that the learner has to handle the following components when using language: the formal system (lexis, morphology, syntax, phonology); the sociolinguistic system (rules of use); and the semantic system (notions, concepts, and logical relations). In order to manipulate the sociolinguistic system efficiently, one needs to know the rules of use; in order to convey semantic meaning, one must know the rules of discourse, which govern what information is presented and how it is arranged. Strategic skills that are required to avoid difficulties or breakdown in communication are somewhat different, being nonlinguistic (see pp. 19–22).

Rules of use

Knowing the rules of use of a language means knowing what utterances are appropriate in a particular sociocultural context, both with respect to meanings that one may convey and to the forms one may use in conveying them. These three factors in verbal communication – appropriateness, meaning, and form – exist in a dynamic relationship. Once one is engaged in verbal communication (oral or written, productive or receptive), all three are important; all three are in play.

An individual using his first language, or a second language that he knows very well, generally pays more conscious attention to appropriateness and meaning than to linguistic form. Someone using a second language that he does not know very well will often pay a very great deal of attention to form, compromise on meaning, and be able to cope with the question of appropriateness minimally if at all. Exactly what classroom teaching can do about teaching the rules of use became a major preoccupation during the 1970s. Concern with appropriate language use had sometimes been present before, of course, but was often absent: For example, in structure-based teaching it is seldom revealed *at the same time* as the imperative forms of verbs are being taught that they are seldom used to convey polite requests. In other words, rules of use (and of discourse), as well as rules of grammar, influence the choice of form.

In order to be clear about why and how ideas on appropriateness came to gain importance in applied linguistics and in classroom teaching, we need to examine a number of changes in teaching and in linguistics that have occurred in recent years. For decades now, the characteristics of the total population of second language learners have been changing. The sheer number of people wanting instruction is enormous today. The educational base has broadened, and adult education is seen as a necessity and even a basic right. There have also been large population shifts, sometimes the result of international conflict, sometimes the result of international cooperation. Large numbers of adult immigrants, migrant workers, and their children all require second language learning opportunities. Finally, travel abroad on business and on holiday has become standard practice for vast numbers of people. All of these changes have increased the pressure on language teachers and language planners to produce more efficient courses, more interesting opportunities for learning. Methods based principally on teaching linguistic structures could no longer do the job for the new clientele.

A different model for second language course design was therefore required: one that would take into account the particular aims of particular learners, as well as their educational backgrounds and other characteristics. Work in second language acquisition has centered on the learner as individual and on the psychological aspects of interaction. Changes in learning theory have had considerable impact on approaches to language teaching, and the need to influence learners' affective involvement in the process is now taken for granted.[1] Sociolinguistic approaches have produced similar concern for the process of language learning as well as the product, but by a different route. It is this route that I want to trace briefly in two parts, one on language functions, the other on discourse analysis.

This division also reflects two phases of work in syllabus design for second language teaching. In North America, the term "syllabus" is often used interchangeably with "curriculum." However, I would like to preserve the distinction proposed by Robertson (1971: 566): "The curriculum includes the goals, objectives, content, processes, resources, and means of evaluation of all the learning experiences planned for pupils both in and out of the school and community through classroom instruction and related programs." He defines syllabus as "a statement of the plan for any part of the curriculum, excluding the element of curriculum evaluation itself." This distinction is particularly useful if one considers that language courses are often given by private individuals,

---

1 Since the focus of this book is primarily on sociocultural dimensions of second language course design, work in second language acquisition theory will not be reviewed here. Davies, Criper and Howatt (1984: Part 4), Hyltenstam and Pienemann (1985), and Lightbown (1985) all contain full and up-to-date discussion of second language acquisition theory and its relation to language teaching.

or by groups that are not part of any educational institution. Especially in ESL, such courses are commonplace, so that a syllabus that defines a language course as a whole or in parts (e.g., goals, objectives, resources ...) for a group of learners meeting entirely outside an institutional setting is a very useful tool. (See Yalden 1983 and Brumfit 1984c for further discussion of the concept of syllabus.)

Reorienting language teaching

A number of different attempts have been made to provide a theoretical base for reorienting language teaching, of which some are more radical than others. One of the most influential has been the Council of Europe Modern Languages Project, widely known through the Threshold Level syllabuses published between 1973 and 1982 (see Coste et al. 1976; Trim et al. 1980; van Ek 1980). Semantic principles of content selection were advanced, notably in Wilkins's contributions to the project and in Wilkins (1976). This work led to a preoccupation in second language teaching, during a period of several years, with the communicative functions of language. Both syllabuses and teaching materials with a heavy emphasis on these functions appeared.

The establishment of the European Economic Community (EEC) triggered the production of a set of proposals for a "unit/credit" system of language teaching for adults (Trim 1980; van Ek 1980). These proposals were drawn up for the Council of Europe by a team of linguists from a number of countries. A central requirement of the project was that a single statement of content should be worked out, which could afterward be actualized or exemplified for each language for which courses were required. Learners would be able to accumulate credits as they worked through one unit after another, and so the system could be used simultaneously in all of the EEC countries. Such an approach would be most immediately useful in teaching learners who would be moving back and forth from one country to another as "guest workers," and who would require rapid training in fairly well-specified areas of second languages for occupational purposes. Other exemplifications would in time be required for other categories of learners. In the course of examining the kind of syllabus that would be required for such courses, Wilkins argued that the numerous pedagogical strategies in existence could be grouped around two conceptually distinct types of approach, labeled "synthetic" and "analytic," and that any actual course or syllabus could be placed somewhere on a continuum between the two. Wilkins defines the first of these two strategies as follows:

A synthetic language-teaching strategy is one in which the different parts of language are taught separately and step-by-step so that acquisition is a process of gradual accumulation of the parts until the whole structure of the language has been built up. (Wilkins 1976: 2)

In planning courses based on this approach, the language items to be taught are ordered in a list of grammatical structures and lexical items. The learner is exposed at any one time only to a limited sample of the target language, and the sample is carefully controlled by the teaching situation. The learner's job is thus to resynthesize language that has been taken apart and presented to him in small pieces; and this synthesis generally takes place only in the "advanced" levels of learning. When examined by these criteria, the Grammar-Translation and Audiolingual methods both belong in the synthetic category.

The analytic approach is intended to lead to communicative competence in a broader sense, rather than to linguistic competence alone. In this kind of approach, based on meaning, one relies to a far greater extent than in a structural approach on the learner's capacity to analyze language for himself. The problem of putting an analytic approach into practice, as it was first seen, is largely one of finding a way to express what it is that people do with language, so that the unavoidable process of limitation or selection can take place (Wilkins 1976: 13). This representation of the process of syllabus construction led to further examination of the functions of language and to work in needs analysis, in order to determine the purposes for which people learn language and the kind of language performance needed to attain those purposes.

The semantic syllabus

Wilkins (1976) had offered a new model for language syllabuses, springing from a definition of meaning that is central to functional theories of language: that the meaning of an utterance derives from the *whole situation* in which language is used, and not from words or sentences in isolation. From this principle it follows that meaning must be approached through the study of language in use, language in discourse. To approach language in this way leads directly to the study of the functions of language and their relation to grammatical forms. It leads also to the use of notions, functions, settings, topics, and so on, in syllabus design — as well as to the use of the forms of language.

So it is that in applied linguistics and in language teaching, an important concern during the 1970s and 1980s has been the application of functional theories to syllabus design. Wilkins's distinction between the synthetic approach (leading to the goal of linguistic perfection) and the analytic one (leading to the goal of communicative competence) has had significant effects. He proposed three components for semantic syllabuses based on the analytic approach (Wilkins 1976: 21–2):

- the semantic (basic concepts, *what* to communicate)
- the functional (interactional aspect, *why* we communicate)
- the formal (grammatical knowledge, *how* we communicate).

The semantic aspect of meaning had been given more or less emphasis according to one's approach to language teaching. In the classic Grammar-Translation Method, for example, works of great authors were often used as texts, and emphasis was placed on the ideas in these texts. In the Audiolingual Method, although structures were vastly more important than anything else, the semantic content was usually drawn from some aspect of life in the target environment. The interactional aspect of meaning, the use of language to do things, had not been at all central in language teaching. The very basis of a functional approach to language teaching, however, derives from the conviction that what people want to do through language is more important than mastery of the language as an unapplied system.

Many attempts have been made to work out new types of syllabus based on an analytic approach. One of the most discussed has been the functional syllabus. In this connection, it is important to remember, as Wilkins has stated, that "it is . . . possible to think in terms of a *functional syllabus* and a *conceptual syllabus,* although only a syllabus that covered both functional (and modal) and conceptual categories would be a fully *notional syllabus*)" (1976: 24). It is clear, then, that by the mid-70s, three different orientations to second language teaching (linguistic, functional, conceptual) had been defined. It is also possible to see that the definition of three kinds of meaning and three kinds of syllabus could be interpreted as meaning that one or other might be used to the total exclusion of the others. It is equally clear, however, that this was never intended to be the interpretation: The three components advanced by Wilkins and discussed by many other linguists are not separable. The question is one of emphasis, not of separation, in course design and language teaching.

Language functions

Before going on, in Part III, to look at various proposals for dealing with these and other components in language teaching, it will be helpful to summarize briefly some important work that has profoundly affected the concept of the functions of language. In this context, we must stress again that the concept of second language proficiency can be examined from *two* theoretical perspectives: one concerned with the process the individual undergoes in learning a second language, the other with what it means to become a user of the second language. The two are complementary, and both have to be taken into consideration in course design. It is the latter, which is based on functional theories of language, and which has been of more central concern in European than in North American approaches to language and to language teaching, that is under discussion in this chapter. I return to the other in Chapter 4.

Philosophers, anthropologists, sociologists, and linguists have all produced theories concerning the link between speech and its context. From the early years of the century, each of these disciplines has examined the problem of language, thought, and meaning from its own vantage point. In order to understand fully the premises on which notional syllabus design (or communicative syllabus design as it was later termed[2]) is based, it is helpful to know something about these cross-disciplinary currents. In linguistics, Ferdinand de Saussure recognized functional aspects of language in distinguishing two levels of language: *langue* and *parole*. However, he was convinced that *langue* was the proper object of study of scientific linguistics, and that *langue* was *forme:* The study of language use and the context of language was to be left to the philosophers. Chomsky, as we have noted, also placed constraints on the scientific study of linguistics which similarly exclude context. The American structuralists as well were primarily concerned with form. The reasons for the exclusion or deemphasis of context are different in each case, but the result has been the same: to leave the effect of context on language to be studied by other disciplines.

Yet anyone involved with applied linguistics and language teaching can hardly avoid noticing many references to the contexts of language use, and to "speech acts." How did such ideas find their way into these fields? Through certain schools of linguistics in Europe, for one, in which the relationship between language and the context of its use had not been excluded; from philosophy; and from anthropology and sociology as well. These disciplines all meet in the study of language as communication – or pragmatics.

The Oxford English Dictionary gives one of the meanings of "pragmatic" as "dealing with matters according to their practical significance or immediate importance." In linguistics, "pragmatics" has a technical meaning. It is one of the three branches of semiotics, which in turn is the systematic study of linguistic *and nonlinguistic* signs, and which has been elaborated by many disciplines: philosophy, psychology, sociology, anthropology, linguistics. From a philosophical point of view, semiotics comprises:

2 It has been said that the term "communicative" cannot be used of "syllabus," but only of the methodology used to implement the syllabus (Widdowson 1984: 26). If the definition of syllabus I have given is accepted, and if it includes processes and resources, it is legitimate to use "communicative syllabus" to mean that *all parts* of the syllabus will be based on a view of language as communication.

- *pragmatics:* the study of how signs and symbols are used by humans for communicating in a particular language
- *semantics:* the study of the relationships between the "symbol" and its "referent"
- *syntactics:* the study of symbols in relation to each other
                                                    (Hartmann and Stock 1972: 205)

Studies of how signs and symbols are used for communicating in a particular language can be carried out from a number of perspectives. Let us consider the matter from the vantage point of ethnography. As we have already observed, sociocultural contexts provide constraints on language use (and also clues to correct interpretations of utterances). Descriptions of the components of a "speech event" (a term introduced by Hymes 1967) have been very widely discussed and applied, since it is hypothesized that different sorts of speech events (private conversation, public lectures, political speeches, and so on) have different rules of language use. All of the following have been suggested as components of a speech event at one time or another by ethnographers and others (see, e.g., Jakobson 1960; Hymes 1972; Munby 1978; Canale and Swain 1980):

Participants: speaker/hearer, sender/receiver, etc.
Social relationships, or "role sets"
Setting: in physical time and space
Scene: psychological or cultural setting
Form: linguistic description of the message
Topic: what the message is about
Speech acts or verbal acts
Purpose: goal or intention
Key: serious or mocking, etc.
Genre: casual speech, poem, form letter, etc.
Channel: oral or written
Code: language or variety of a language
Norms of interaction: loudness of voice, physical distance, etc.
Norms of interpretation: how norms of interaction or violation of them
    are interpreted

Note that linguistic form is only one in a long list. Although there are still problems with the theory of the speech event (see, e.g., Canale and Swain 1980 for discussion), the concept has become important in linguistics and has had a significant effect on the reorientation of language teaching.

The speech event has also been seen as encompassing a series of speech acts. From the point of view of linguistic form, grammarians have regularly made it clear that sentences can be statements – or questions or exclamations or commands or wishes, and so on. Philosophers had been traditionally concerned with "statements," which "describe" or "state some fact." These statements could be proved to be either true or false – the business of logicians in particular. However, one of the leading philosophers of this century, J. L. Austin (1962), drew attention to certain arguments to the effect that philosophers had made the mistake of taking as straightforward statements of fact utterances that were either nonsensical or else *intended as something quite different*. He pointed out that these arguments were producing a revolution in philosophy, a revolution that yielded a new area which came to be known as "philosophy of language." Indeed Austin's own work together with that of other philosophers on language as rule-governed *intentional* behavior has also had a dramatic impact on linguistics. (For full discussions on philosophy of language see Austin 1962 and Searle 1969; for its implications for language teaching see Munby 1978; Brumfit and Johnson 1979; Yalden 1983.)

The intentions that a speaker has in making utterances, which do not necessarily coincide with grammatical labels for linguistic forms, now came under increased scrutiny. The idea that language is used to do things, and that the meaning of forms used to accomplish such acts is highly dependent on sociocultural context, had already been introduced into the discussion of linguistic meaning by Malinowski (1923) and Firth (1968). Exactly what the "things" are that one can do with language – that is, the functions of language – had also been an important topic in linguistics since the 1920s and 1930s. The term "language functions" has been used in applied linguistics to refer more frequently to the communicative, interpersonal dimensions of language than to the more purely expressive ones. That the philosophers' speech acts overlap the applied linguists' communicative functions has been thoroughly discussed (e.g., Candlin 1973: 59). It should be noted, though, that the speech act includes the three categories of locutionary acts (the act of saying something with propositional or conceptual meaning), illocutionary acts (the act performed in saying something, and connected with intent), and perlocutionary acts (the effect that arises in a hearer as a result of an illocutionary act). The illocutionary act, the act of *doing* something in saying something, has recently been of greatest interest in applied linguistics.[3]

Austin's lectures and John R. Searle's later elaboration of the theory

---

3 Certain conditions must obtain for an illocutionary act to be performed at all. They are known as "felicity conditions." Austin introduced the concept in his discussion of "performatives" – utterances that are not "statements," in that they are neither true nor false, but are words used to *do* something (e.g., *I bet, I pronounce you man and wife, I promise*, and so on). The felicity conditions have to do with what people expect of each other, appropriateness, and so on. See Austin (1962: 14–15).

of speech acts (Searle 1969) presented a very large range of possibilities to be considered. It is not likely that a definitive list of speech acts will be drawn up for English, let alone one that would be universal, applicable to all languages. The number of such acts, the shades of meaning that can be conveyed, is immense. Furthermore, comparing inventories of speech acts that have been proposed, and contrasting them with other inventories of the communicative functions of language used in applied linguistics (e.g., Munby 1978; van Ek 1980), would serve no useful purpose here. Nevertheless, the *concept* of the speech act and the idea that speech acts are inherent in language have been most valuable for the development of approaches to meaning and to language functions in applied linguistics and second language teaching.

In particular, the work of the British linguist M. A. K. Halliday has contributed a distinctive quality to the interpretations of functional theory in applied linguistics. His theory of language acquisition as mastery of linguistic functions – learning the uses of language and the *meaning-potential* associated with them – has had a great impact.[4] One needs to ask what the functions of language are that the human being masters in order to be able to "mean." Halliday lists seven functions in his study of language development in the child (1975). He states that adult language is far more complex, and that each adult utterance serves *more than one function* at a time. He reduces the enormous functional diversity of adult language usage to a set of only three functional components, which he calls "macro-functions." These are:

– the *interpersonal* function: to establish, maintain and specify relations between members of societies
– the *ideational* function: to transmit information between members of societies
– the *textual* function: to provide texture, the organization of discourse as relevant to the situation.

Both grammarians and philosophers appear to have been examining the ideational function to the exclusion of the others. But each of these components makes a contribution to meaning, and for Halliday it is the *social* functions of language that determine the available meaning options and their structural realizations.

---

4 "Meaning potential" is a central concept in Halliday's work. It is part of his functional theory of language: "Only recently has language acquisition come to be seen as the mastery of linguistic functions, and it is this perspective that is needed here, in which learning language is learning the uses of language and the meaning potential associated with them; the structures, the words and the sounds are the realization of this meaning potential. Learning language is learning to mean" (Kress 1976: 8).

Functions in language teaching

These are complicated ideas, and the fact that scholars working from a number of different disciplines are all contributing to their development does not make it any easier to follow the discussion. They are, however, important and fruitful ideas, which were taken up with great enthusiasm in the 1970s. For a time it seemed that language teaching could be much more closely oriented to learners' needs or aims by analyzing the speech events they were involved in when using the target language, breaking those speech events up into speech acts or language functions, and then teaching the linguistic forms that were appropriate to realize the function within a given speech event. (See Tables 3.1 and 3.2.) Indeed, many courses were built around this idea, especially in the field of language teaching for specific purposes (described in greatest detail by Munby 1978). A spate of books and course materials appeared labeled "functional," built around units with names like "Making Introductions," "Having an Argument," "Polite Requests," "Asking Directions," and so on.[5] In fact many fresh techniques, such as role play, simulations, and exercises taken from drama classes, were introduced into the second language classroom, in an effort to cope with language functions. All this has been refreshing and useful in enriching the possibilities open to the teacher who wants to provide varied and interesting activities for the classroom.

At the same time, however, the detailed specification of linguistic forms to be used for specific communicative functions has turned out to be of limited usefulness. In particular, it was not the solution to the problems of second language course design that had been hoped for. Almost as soon as Wilkins's work on notional syllabuses and the Council of Europe's Threshold Level syllabus for English appeared, there were criticisms of those who attempted to build courses that depended on teaching language functions as their core. The chief allegation was that they fell into the same error as those who had tried to build courses only upon

---

5 For many teachers, the labels of *functional* language teaching are confusingly like *situations*. I have not discussed the situational approach to course design separately, since to do so would require a more extensive treatment of the history of language teaching than is appropriate here. The use of the term "situational" has changed over time: compare, for example, Hornby's description (1950) to Wilkins's comments on it (1976: 15–18). The position it occupies relative to the three major approaches discussed here depends on how it is defined. Wilkins suggests that "it seems best ... to retain the term *situation* for the sum of the observable and independently describable features of the context in which a language event occurs." A situation thus defined is extralinguistic (compare also Halliday et al. 1964: 207), whereas the speech event is entirely linguistic, although influenced by extralinguistic variables.

TABLE 3.1 FUNCTION TO FORM

Function	Sentence forms	Realization
Giving orders	(a) Imperative	"Please go now."
	(b) Conditional	"Perhaps it would be preferable if you went now."
	(c) Infinitive	"I expect you to go now."
	(d) Modal	"You must go now."
	(e) Participial	"You should be going now."

Source: Based on Yalden (1983: 40).

TABLE 3.2 FORM TO FUNCTION

Sentence form	Realization	Function
Imperative	(a) "Give me some water."	Giving orders
	(b) "Release me now."	Pleading
	(c) "Buy Canada Savings Bonds."	Advising
	(d) "Don't go in there."	Warning
	(e) "Try this one on."	Suggesting

Source: Based on Yalden (1983: 40).

structural aspects of meaning. In both cases, the other components of meaning had been thrust aside, and in particular, the textual component had been neglected or ignored. It remained for work in discourse analysis to restore this dimension to course design.

4 Discourse analysis and course design

In this chapter, I will discuss the notion of discourse and try to characterize the domain of discourse analysis from three perspectives: that of linguistics, of second language acquisition research, and of language education. I will then consider briefly several subfields of discourse analysis and their contributions to second language teaching. Finally I will relate this work to course design.

Discourse and discourse analysis

In making proposals with respect to second language learning and teaching today, it is more or less taken for granted that attention must be paid to the use of grammatical forms in the learner's speech or writing *as well as* to the learner's ability to match structures with communicative functions. In other words, the need to be able to use language that is appropriate to the social context has become a central focus for teachers and researchers. The ways in which illocutionary acts are expressed and arranged in sequences (speech events), the roles that participants in such events can take on, and the sociocultural or situational constraints on the options that are available have all been studied in the development of contemporary approaches to language teaching. All this work has also greatly enriched what is known about second language learning.

Nevertheless, using a language (whether first or second) involves something that goes beyond the acquisition of structures and the ability to make appropriate choices in the realization of particular language functions. It also depends crucially on the ability to produce utterances that fit or make sense within a given stretch of discourse, and the ability to interpret the meaning of utterances thus produced by others.

There are things to be clarified here. The first is the use of "utterance" instead of "sentence." Most natural discourse, especially spoken discourse, is unplanned. It is full of false starts, hesitations, partial sentences, phrases not completed, and the like. Anyone who has ever listened to recordings of natural conversation cannot help but be struck by the fact that so much is in the form of what grammarians call incomplete sentences. Moreover, even in informal writing (notes to friends, to oneself, casual letters, and in lecture notes), the same incomplete sentences occur.

39

The term "utterance" has therefore been adopted to describe what people actually say or write in connected discourse. Whether they are actually complete sentences or not does not matter – the term covers both instances as well as single words, sounds such as "uh-huh" which convey meaning but may not be found in the dictionary, and so on.

The second is the importance of context in interpreting ideational or propositional meaning as well as functional meaning. As Widdowson has pointed out, we do not usually engage, in normal linguistic behavior, in the production of separate utterances, one after another, which bear no relation to each other. Rather, they are *used for the creation of discourse*. What does this mean? As Austin and Searle have shown, when people speak or write they express a proposition (a statement, an assertion about something or other), and at the same time they perform an illocutionary act (requesting, refusing, approving, insisting, and so on). This illocutionary act may or may not be specified, but it is always performed. We are *always* speaking (or writing) intentionally.

However, there are also many different ways of *organizing* the information expressed in a proposition, and of placing the propositions in sequence, as well as many different purposes one might have in expressing it in the first place. Put another way, in discourse there are many things going on at once; and the participants have to interpret all aspects of the utterances made by other participants, and provide their own contributions to the process of negotiating meaning – which is what discourse is. This requires more than a display of knowledge of linguistic rules, for meaning does not reside in words alone. Words are used in conventional and unconventional ways to create the meanings that people engaged in discourse wish to convey.

> We are generally required to use our knowledge of the language system in order to achieve some kind of communicative purpose. That is to say, we are generally called upon to produce instances of language *use:* we do not simply manifest the abstract system of the language [as instances of *usage*], we at the same time realize it as meaningful communicative behaviour. (Widdowson 1978: 3)

Analysis of this "meaningful communicative behavior" has become a major preoccupation in linguistics as well as in sociology, ethnography, and other fields concerned with communication. Within the area of second language teaching, there are several perspectives that are of interest: the linguistic, the psycholinguistic, and the educational.

A linguistic perspective

Although analysis limited to the internal workings of verbal language (phonology, morphology, syntax) is the central core of the discipline of linguistics, interest in the *process* of communication, whereby we create, negotiate, and interpret personal meanings, requires investigation. Under pressure from many domains, but especially from sociology and ethnology,

> there has been a widening of the field of research to include the external functioning of the verbal code as well, what people *do* with words. The emphasis in such an approach shifts from structure and grammar to function and communicative competence, from assembling sentences to doing things with utterances, from the sentence in isolation to the utterance in context. This, then, is the domain of discourse analysis ... the description of the process whereby we create and relate, organize and realize meaning. (Riley 1985: 1–2)

According to Riley, there is plainly a distinction between the grammar of sentences and another kind of grammar, which is concerned with the pragmatic use of language and is now referred to as *text grammar*. In his view, the study and analysis of discourse belongs in this domain. However, other linguists argue that distinctions between semantics and pragmatics and between "sentence" grammar and "text" grammar cannot be maintained, and that the study of discourse must involve a study of every aspect of language (Crombie 1985: vii). If this argument is accepted, discourse analysis becomes an overarching discipline for all study of language.

These are interesting theoretical arguments, but it is not our purpose to try to resolve them here. We should turn instead to other areas that touch on second language teaching more closely, in particular second language acquisition research and language education.

Second language acquisition research: a fresh approach

In second language acquisition, as in linguistics, attention remained focused for a long time on syntax. Studies of error analysis, for example, were entirely based on the examination of the acquisition of structures by second language learners.

Until quite recently, the learner's need to acquire pragmatic knowledge (the ability to choose language that is appropriate to the context) and knowledge of the rules of discourse had not been investigated. The nature of the language input that the child or the second language learner receives and the interaction between input and production had also not been examined. With expanding interest in the process as well as the product of language acquisition, and in the social functions of language, a fresh approach to research design was needed, and it was suggested that discourse analysis represented an approach that would allow the researcher to study all the relevant factors in second language acquisition

(Larsen-Freeman 1980). The amount of work that has been carried out since 1980 under this rubric is very large, and the whole field is now broken down into subfields (cf. Larsen-Freeman 1980; Stubbs 1983). It is beginning to have a considerable impact on second language teaching, especially since one of those subfields deals directly with language in the classroom and teacher–student exchanges.

Language education and discourse analysis

Discourse analysis also contributes theoretical constructs that are directly useful in second language teaching. Widdowson, for example, recently introduced the term "capacity" instead of "communicative competence" for language education, on the grounds that "competence" refers to what the grammarian *represents* as language knowledge, but not to the language user's mode of knowing (Widdowson 1983: 23). Capacity is defined as "the ability to use a knowledge of language as a resource for the creation of meaning" (p. 25). There is good reason to accept this distinction between communicative competence and capacity; but even if one sets it aside for the moment, it is essential to note that Widdowson insists that capacity cannot be accounted for in models of grammar, since it is not the linguist's task to set up models for the representation of competence that is nonlinguistic.

What is needed, for language education, is a model of language use that accounts for the essential features of the discourse process, rather than simply atomizing the user's behavior into components of communicative competence. Widdowson has developed a model for this purpose (1983: chap. 2), in which the concept of the *schema* is central. Schemata relate to all human extraction of meaning from sensory data. They are said to be complex knowledge structures (which may be conventional or habitual), which function as "ideational scaffolding" in the organization and interpretation of experience (Brown and Yule 1983: 247–8). In the field of discourse analysis, they "can be seen as the organised background knowledge which leads us to *expect* or predict aspects in our interpretation of discourse" (Brown and Yule 1983: 248).

Widdowson defines the schema as "a stereotypic pattern derived from instances of past experience which organizes language in preparation for use" (1983: 37). Schemata, in this sense, can be thought of in two ways: in relation to the propositional content of discourse – that is, as frames of reference – and in relation to the illocutionary content, as rhetorical routines. Both have to be established through negotiation, since people are impelled to "put their schemata into contact with others" (Widdowson 1983: 47) using procedures that Widdowson describes.

Widdowson's procedures are based on Grice's work on the "cooperative principle," much referred to in discourse analysis. Grice identified four maxims as constituents of this principle:

Quantity: Make your contribution as informative as possible. Do not be more informative than required.

Quality: Do not say what you believe to be false. Do not say that for which you lack adequate evidence.

Relation: Be relevant.

Manner: Be perspicuous. Avoid obscurity and ambiguity. Be brief, orderly, and polite.

(Grice 1975: 45)

Grice's principle has been frequently used in the analysis of how propositional information is conveyed, and the concept of negotiation of meaning is based on it also. Although Grice's maxims appear to be very simple, applying them to the interpretation of meaning is not. Since the relationship between propositions is not always signaled overtly in discourse, participants have to infer these relations. They therefore have to make assumptions about the way their interlocutors organize discourse, and Grice's maxims are proposed as providing the basis for such assumptions. These maxims as well as Searle's "felicity conditions" must be followed in order for the conversation or written interaction to work – that is, in order that the participants may understand each other. The procedures that participants use to infer relations among propositions are *interpretive,* and supply meanings and underlying pattern even when they are not obvious from the surface content of the discourse. The language user thus becomes able to anticipate the development of discourse and to make sense of it. Knowledge of these procedures and how they are used would be enormously useful in second language acquisition research and in language teaching, hence the interest in this kind of approach to discourse analysis.

Subfields of discourse analysis

In order to discover what the structure of discourse may be, and to analyze it, it has been necessary to attempt the identification of units of discourse. There have been a variety of constituent units proposed, often arranged into hierarchies. The description frequently begins with the context: job interview, committee meeting, doctor/patient interviews, and more recently, the classroom. Speech events such as arguments, telling a story or a joke, or transactions of various sorts can be considered in sequence within a context, or can be analyzed on their own. The communicative acts – or functional units – involved can also be identified. As a result, several different approaches to description and analysis of units and levels of units have been developed.

Conversational analysis

One very large area of research is concerned with spoken interaction and is known as *conversational analysis*. Among studies of conversations carried on in a classroom setting, Coulthard (1977) is considered a classic. Moving from an initial preoccupation with turn-taking, a central concern in this area, he establishes a hierarchical set of units for use in the analysis of classroom interaction. Coulthard's units have been used in many other studies, as they are or with modifications. The lesson consists of transactions, which in turn consist of exchanges, in turn comprising moves (opening, closing, follow-up, with still further subdivisions) themselves made up of acts. The smallest unit, the act, has no structure at the discourse level. Coulthard's acts are not the same as Austin's or Searle's *speech acts,* which were defined in terms of the illocutionary force they carry. Coulthard's acts have to be seen in terms of the relationships they enter into with other discourse functions.

Coulthard's work has led to a great deal of investigation of classroom discourse. Some of the studies in this subfield take a more ethnographic approach: They look at patterns of observed communicative behavior.[1] Within the range of studies of classroom discourse as such, however, a question that has received much attention is how far it deviates from natural discourse. This has to be resolved before one can deal with the further question of *what kind* of linguistic environment (natural? structured?) should be provided for the learner. In this regard, work on *communication strategies* has been growing – an area that is sometimes regarded as peripheral or separate from discourse analysis (see Chapter 2). Initially, communication strategies were regarded as "a systematic attempt by the learner to express or decode meaning in the target language, in situations where the appropriate systematic TL rules have not been formed" (Tarone, Frauenfelder, and Selinker 1976). This definition clearly relates studies of communication strategies to studies of interlanguage. Recently, however, the definition has been broadened to relate the term to "a mutual attempt of two interlocutors to agree on a meaning in situations where requisite meaning structures [linguistic and sociolinguistic] do not seem to be shared" (Tarone 1983: 65) – a definition that brings the area clearly into the same field as discourse analysis, with its emphasis on negotiation of meaning.

1 See Agar (1980) for an introduction to ethnography, and Stubbs (1983) for a description of the approach in language teaching.

Discourse features

Another approach to discourse analysis concerns itself with *discourse features,* including connectives and other linguistic devices of cohesion (Halliday and Hasan 1976). Discourse "markers" (such as "next," "finally," "on the other hand") that signal the arrangement of meaning in the text have been described and categorized for English, and the descriptions have been much used in the teaching of reading and writing, and in devising materials for teaching students to take lecture notes (e.g., Young and Fitzgerald 1982).

Coherence

Since the organization of meaning in text is not always signaled overtly, studies of *discourse coherence* have also become extremely important in discourse analysis. The way different communicative acts combine to produce understandable stretches of discourse, how the participants in discourse are able to interpret it as being coherent even when it is not from the point of view of grammatical cohesion, and the role of context in establishing coherence are all central problems (see, e.g., Widdowson 1978).

Analysis of cohesion and coherence in scientific and technical texts has contributed considerably to course design for specific-purpose groups. In the course of such analysis, further units have been proposed, reminiscent of rhetoricians' categories. The rhetorical functions of definition; description and classification; rhetorical relations of time order, space order, and causality; as well as rhetorical features, such as the interpretation of illustrations and the rhetoric of instructions (found, for example, in technical manuals), have all come under investigation. (See, e.g., Lackstrom, Selinker, and Trimble 1973; Allen and Widdowson 1974a; Selinker, Tarone, and Hanzeli 1981.) What the rhetorical functions are, how they are sequenced, and the forms of their linguistic realizations (i.e., the relationship of rhetoric and grammar) are questions that interest linguists working in this area (Lackstrom et al. 1973; Selinker and Trimble 1974; Selinker, Todd Trimble, and Trimble 1978). For example, Todd Trimble and Trimble advance the idea that "the basic rhetorical functions found most commonly in English for Specific Purposes discourse are fundamental elements in the organization of the presentation of information (fact or hypothesis) and that a clear recognition and understanding of these functions – and the grammar and lexis used to present them – are necessary to a full comprehension of ESP discourse" (1982: 213). The model they present is concerned primarily with (1) the rhetoric of description, definition, classification, instructions, and the visual-verbal relationship; (2) the grammar of modal verb forms, passive and stative verb forms, nontemporal use of tense, and the use of the definite article; and (3) lexis relating to subtechnical terms and noun compounds. This kind of research has provided the basis for discourse-based approaches to teaching scientific and technical English, as well as general English (see, e.g., Allen and Widdowson 1974b; Widdowson 1979).

Contrastive studies

Whether or not discourse units are universal across languages or confined to single languages or groups of languages has become a current concern (e.g., Fraser 1978; Thomas 1983; Wolfson 1983). In language teaching it has long been known that lack of knowledge of appropriate forms for the realization of speech acts can cause communication problems, for example, using only "please" when something more elaborate is called for ("Would you please"), or saying "thanks" when "many thanks for helping me" would be appropriate. Recently, however, the structure of entire speech events has been examined with a view to determining whether misunderstandings or communication breakdowns may not occur as a result of differing cultural patterns – with interesting and revealing results (Akinnaso and Ajirotutu 1982; Gumperz and Cook-Gumperz 1982).

The rhetorical structure of written text may also differ considerably from one language to another. If the differences can be determined, language teaching will certainly be influenced. Kaplan has named this area *contrastive rhetoric* and has carried out numerous studies based on this hypothesis (e.g., Kaplan 1972, 1978, 1983). The research has already been applied, especially in the teaching of reading and writing.[2]

Discourse analysis and course design

Discourse analysis, however defined, is quite evidently the meeting place for many types of research and many interests. I have touched briefly on some of these areas, in particular those that have begun to have an effect on approaches to language teaching and on classroom practice. The proliferation of perspectives, complicated by the new terminology used to describe units of discourse, may produce a strong desire in the reader to retreat to the security of the structure-based course. However,

---

2 There has been recently (in North America at any rate) an enormous growth of interest in traditional rhetoric in mother tongue teaching of English, and at least one conference devoted to bringing together experts in both mother tongue and second language areas. See Freedman and Pringle (1980) and Freedman et al. (1983).

it is premature to sound the alarm, for there are many reasons to pursue this approach to the examination of the nature of discourse.

By the mid-1970s, development of the functional-notional approach to syllabus design had been received as a major advance in language teaching. But attempts to implement it in preparing second language courses soon received severe criticism. Problems arose when the inter-relation of all the categories that had been proposed (objectives, general notions, topics, functions, forms) were attempted, even though they could be considered *additional*, rather than alternative, criteria for course design (Strevens 1977: 25). Candlin identified the chief difficulty: "an item-bank of speech-acts ... cannot serve any more than sentences as the direct end point of a communicative syllabus" (1976: 252). He went on to suggest that we expect learners to do three things: to produce grammatically well-formed sentences and to be aware of intrasentential semantic identity; to recognize and produce pragmatically equivalent utterances; *and* to "manage" the interaction. Instruction in grammar will provide for the first ability; the second requires some awareness of the communicative functions of language and of varieties of language, register, style, and the like. The new categories that had been proposed for the notional syllabus, added to those already used in a grammatical syllabus, would provide for these two abilities, as long as a way could be found to interrelate them in preparing classroom materials and activities. But the third ability – managing interaction – had not been taken into account at all, and without it the course designer could not go beyond the stage of phrasebook language.

This criticism brings the debate on course design squarely into the area of discourse analysis. One of the early responses to the problem is contained in *Un niveau seuil* (Coste et al. 1976), the actualizations in French of the notions, functions, and so on that underlie the entire Threshold concept. In addition to intentional acts, it distinguishes others that serve the discourse function of initiating and responding. It also includes functions that relate to the discourse itself. *Un niveau seuil* is more than a version, for French, of *Threshold Level for English* – it adds a vital element to the concept of the notional syllabus. Munby's (1978) taxonomy of language skills is largely a list of skills needed to process discourse.

As long as discourse functions are presented as another component of a syllabus, however, the problem of developing the ability to manage interactions still has not been dealt with. It is interesting to note that both psychological and sociological views of second language learning and teaching converge on this point. Recent psycholinguistic theory suggests that language acquisition is more organic than learned (Corder 1978), and that more effective second language learning will take place if the emphasis is on getting one's meaning across or understanding one's interlocutor rather than on formal accuracy. Sociolinguistic theory suggests that second language teaching programs should be approached from the starting point of language needs and the kinds of meanings we can express through language rather than that of *a priori* analysis of the target language. Both points of view come together in the field of discourse analysis.

Where practice is concerned, it is a matter of deciding how much language teaching can be expected to do. It has been said that teachers must be concerned with "who says what, when, where, how and why." This would mean attention to roles (teacher, student, doctor, patient) and interactions (superior to inferior? equals?) – in other words *who* – as well as to surface semantic content in the forms of topics and notions (*what*), the influence of temporal and physical setting (*when* and *where*), linguistic form and medium, mode, and channel (*how*), and intent (*why*). In addition, one still has to consider how what is uttered forms coherent discourse, and how one can interpret it.

All of this brings us back to the notion of communicative competence, which cannot be considered without a knowledge of speech act theory, functional theories of language, ethnographic approaches, and discourse analysis. If using language involves the ability to participate in meaningful discourse, and if the goal of second language teaching is to assist the learner to use the language, then how does the teacher intervene in the development of this ability?

Since the mid-1970s, there have been various responses to this question, resulting in an interesting debate on the issue and proposals for a number of models for syllabus design. It is to this debate that I turn in Part III; in Part IV, I will suggest a framework for course design that represents a concrete response to the problems at hand.

Part III From theory to practice

The traditional role of the teacher has been put in question in the contemporary literature, and the nature of second language teaching is being reexamined, quite possibly with a view to a complete redefinition.

This section sets forth a number of reflections on the teacher as teacher, and on the content and process of teaching. The links between teachers, linguists, and learners can be interpreted from several perspectives; some of these are identified, and a number of models for language teaching, implying various types of collaborative or independent relationships, are discussed. Finally, the teacher's role in designing second language courses is examined, and a concrete procedure that leads to the production of frameworks for courses is presented.

5 Teachers and teaching

Perceptions of the language teacher's role have changed considerably since the 1930s. Language teachers are no longer seen exclusively as individuals who hold and transmit language (like any other teacher), but as people who assist the learner to develop a natural capacity to communicate in another language.

Waves of change

I will look first at two influential conceptions of what the language teacher is and what he teaches, which flow from two still-current influences on language teaching: Grammar Translation and behaviorism. I will then look at more recent developments that have produced the approaches known as "communicative." My illustrations are taken from manuals for modern language teaching, because I want to make the point that similar attitudes have prevailed no matter what language was being taught – and also because a distinctive area of second language teaching dealing exclusively with English did not really appear until the 1950s.[1]

The Classical Approach

The curriculum in Spanish at the University of Toronto in the 1920s read as follows:

Second Year: Knapp's Spanish Grammar
Third Year: Knapp's Spanish Grammar
Fourth Year: Grammar; Knapp's Spanish Reading, dictation, composition, translation ....
(Canadian Committee on Modern Languages 1928: 76)

When one compares this starkly simple description with some of today's sophisticated and complicated descriptions of course content, one is

---

1 See Strevens (1985) for a discussion of this difference and its effects on teacher training in particular. Howatt (1984) has an excellent account of the development of English language teaching approaches in the U.K.

51

struck by the clarity of the role that it suggests for the teacher. Fraser and Squair, for example, in their French manual of grammar (published in 1900 and widely used in Canada) certainly do not dwell on the learning process, on individual needs, or on any of the other considerations that teachers and materials writers take for granted now. Theirs is clearly and unequivocally a scholar's manual of grammar. How simple this makes life for teachers, and what an unassailable position they occupy. Language is taught in the same way as logic and literature, and the teachers' main duty is to impart knowledge to sometimes recalcitrant pupils. Harsh lectures to students, with a decidedly moral flavor, are therefore sometimes required. Here is an example taken from a manual of French composition:

Two pieces of advice may fitly be offered at the beginning of this "Junior Manual" of French Composition. One belongs to the moral sphere and concerns the reader's attitude to the study of French.... The most helpful question which a prospective candidate [for the School Certificate] can ask himself is not "shall I pass?" but "shall I *deserve* to pass?" If, as may be hoped, future generations of... boys and girls come to write French more correctly than their predecessors, it will not be by a change of method, but by a change of heart. (Ritchie 1955: 1–2)

Clearly the onus is on the unfortunate student to get on with the job; the teacher is not responsible for foolish errors committed by indolent boys and girls. The relationship between teacher and learner is that of the classical teacher-centered methodology. And what of the content being taught? It is grammar, very often for the sake of reading and of making logical distinctions. An example: A Spanish grammar published in the United States in the 1940s provides a straightforward introduction, reflecting a no-nonsense view of what language teaching and learning is all about. Its authors take a sternly grammatical and highly economical stance. The book "is designed to serve exclusively as a basal textbook for beginners who want to master at the earliest possible date such essentials of Spanish grammar as will permit them to read and understand ordinary Spanish prose" (Hills, Ford, and Rivera 1949: *i*). Teachers are expected to "know the grammar" of the second language and to be able to provide technical explanations, rules, and examples. They are not necessarily required to speak the target language, since their students are not obliged to do so either. The roles of both teacher and student are well defined – and in that context perfectly well understood by society.

Four decades of change

Since the end of World War II, teachers have found themselves under considerable pressure to abandon the long-standing teacher-centered model described above, though it had been in general use in second language teaching since the late eighteenth century. In the teaching of French, for example, a paragraph from a leading publication of the postwar period reads as follows:

We teach a "living" language: a language lives only when it is spoken. . . . From the first words of this preface we want to warn the teacher against the temptation to "teach the book," a temptation inherited from classical pedagogy in which the book often reigns alone, and in which the absence of a printed text plunges teacher and pupils into a state of cruel disarray, or at least causes a certain unease. . . . We are not hostile to teaching through the use of books: we wish only that, in teaching a language, it should come at the right time and place. (CREDIF 1962: *vii;* my translation)

This insistence on setting aside the printed text, and on the independence of the language teacher from the printed word, represents an extraordinary reversal of priorities. In Europe generally, changes that were occurring were based on functional theories of language. In the United Kingdom in particular, Leonard Bloomfield's linguistic theory and B. F. Skinner's views, as expressed in *Verbal Behavior* (1957), were explicitly rejected (Strevens 1985b: 96). Although approaches emphasized contemporary, oral language, they led more directly to what are now known as communicative approaches (Howatt 1984: 272). In the United States and Canada, however, change was heavily influenced by behaviorism. What is more, objectives were now defined in a completely different way. Teachers of language were not to seek equal status with teachers of other subjects, but to proclaim their independence. An illustration of this view can be found in a manual accompanying a Spanish language textbook:

The learning of a modern foreign language has its own objectives and procedures, which tend to be quite different from other academic disciplines to which the student is subject. . . . In his studies, a student is accustomed to using those capacities that depend wholly on conscious intellectual effort (of analysis, synthesis, problem solving, reading, etc.). Such procedures also eventually enter into language learning, particularly at a written level. However, language learning is foremost a habit-forming process similar to learning to play a musical instrument. (Lado and Blansitt 1967: 1)

Though the subject matter was still language structure, the emphasis during the behaviorist period in North America was on the oral medium, and meaning was deemphasized. The way in which students were to learn and practice the subject was to be different also. The teacher of a second language was operating now in a self-contained universe, separated from the rest of the curriculum to a very large degree, and performing a mechanical and relatively passive task as little more than a good model.

This was a period of quite violent change, followed in the 1970s by a spontaneous reaction against extremes of behaviorism in second language teaching. A fresh examination of the learning process and of how to provide for it commenced. The goals of language instruction in the 1960s had been obscured or altered so as to become confined to something rather narrow, and during the decade that followed teachers wanted once again to see more emphasis on meaning, and more flexibility in the use of teaching materials. These desires are reflected in the textbooks and teacher's manuals, which become more adaptable in terms of how much time to allow per lesson, for example, and exhort teachers to incorporate other types of materials into the curriculum.

At all events, the classic and the behaviorist role models for the teacher should be viewed as just that: models. Most classroom teachers have always been eclectic and not prone to accept advice unquestioningly. Nevertheless, these models or types reflect the thinking of linguists and teacher trainers, and have also been approved by our educational systems at various times as the ideals toward which second language teachers should strive. Today, we find another model being proposed, one that requires some very great changes in attitude both toward what to teach and how to teach it. The explanation underlying these changes is complex. Currents of development in applied linguistics and in society, described earlier in Part II, are bringing about further changes and a redefinition of the role and status of the teacher.

Changing perceptions

Changes: the learner at the center

Concurrent with the spontaneous desire of teachers to free themselves from the lock-step approach to second language instruction, and to respond to what they perceive to be the real needs of their students, a large body of empirical research has been carried out that points in the same direction. For example, in their study of the good language learner Naiman et al. comment as follows:

In classroom language learning the use of carefully prepared course materials and the great number of question-and-answer exercises, exclusively directed by the teachers, somehow disguise the fact that the learner should play a part in making decisions and be allowed to exercise personal choice.... The present study suggests that too close, step-by-step direction of language classes may not always produce the desired effect because the learner has too little chance of developing his own learning strategies. (1978: 103)

Recognition of the enormous possible variation in learning styles has thus led to a much more complex view of learner-centered instruction, one that includes choices in four areas: objectives of learning, rate of learning, method (or style) of learning, and content of learning. A definition of this kind points to the necessity for much more teamwork among teachers, and a completely different approach to structuring the curriculum and the timetable, if a learner-centered perspective is considered desirable. The teacher becomes less visibly central as the concept of one method for all learners disappears.

The affective element

Research in second language acquisition leads to another body of theory that is of particular interest in the context of learner-centered instruction and the role the teacher plays therein. "Acquisition" and "learning" have now been given technical definitions, chiefly as a result of Krashen's work. He describes his Monitor Model of second language performance as follows:

> The adult second language performer can 'internalize' rules of a target language via one or both of two separate systems: an implicit way, termed subconscious language *acquisition* and an explicit way, conscious language *learning*. Language acquisition is very similar to the process children use in acquiring first *and second* language. It requires meaningful interaction in the target language, natural communication, in which speakers are not concerned with the form of their utterances but with the messages they are conveying and understanding. Error correction and explicit teaching of rules do not seem to be relevant to language acquisition. . . . Conscious language learning, on the other hand, is said to be helped a great deal by error correction and the presentation of explicit rules. (Krashen 1978: 1–2)

It is interesting to note that Agard, ten years earlier, had stated that "the most . . . that a 'teacher' of violin, or of fencing, or of a language, can do is to surround his pupil with the best possible conditions for his learning and thenceforth to supervise and guide his practice" (Agard 1968: 1). Agard wrote these words for a manual to accompany a textbook of a strongly audiolingual type; yet they seem to forecast the definition of what we take today to be a new role for the second language teacher: facilitator rather than director. Where the experts writing in the late 1960s or early 1970s differ from those writing today seems to be in their view of how to provide the best possible conditions for learning. Although Krashen has elaborated a comprehensive theory which contains a number of elements that would control the conditions for learning, by no means would all researchers agree with his conclusions.[2] The fundamental question of exactly what those conditions are still remains to be answered.

2 See Part IV of this book for further discussion of the learning–acquisition distinction.

Overall, however, we do gain an impression of the teacher as responsible to some extent at least for the affective aspects of learning. On the role of teacher feedback in preventing the fossilized errors of second language learners Brown observes that for communication to take place at all, positive affective feedback is essential. In the act of free and meaningful communication, however, there is very little that can be predicted scientifically. As a result, teachers must be prepared to cope with whatever linguistic forms manifest themselves; they must also be prepared to give positive feedback and to be particularly sensitive to cross-cultural variations in the learner's perception of reinforcers (Brown 1980). Another implication Brown draws from the research is that whatever feedback the teacher provides possesses affective attributes, such as self-esteem, empathy, inhibition, alienation. The teacher must provide support for the student, and avoid being threatening and alienating: a far cry in other words from moral admonitions and terrified pupils.

These notions carry over into the area of error correction and additionally complicate the task of the teacher. Perhaps no correction at all is warranted – in Skinnerian terms, we should only offer positive reinforcement of desired behavior and ignore the undesired. But we have learned from other models and from experience in language teaching that *neutral* feedback can be perceived as a positive reinforcement of the error. Therefore, Brown suggests that "it is the teacher's task to assess all the social, psychological, cultural, and linguistic attributes of a learner's discourse and then to provide appropriate forms of correction" (Brown 1980: 7). A tall order!

The social element

These comments on learner-centered instruction and on second language acquisition research lead toward the current definition of the teacher's role. Second language acquisition theory has suggested that classroom procedures should be oriented toward the communicative situation, and away from conscious and analytical study of structure – though the latter is not necessarily excluded. There is another source of renewal in second language teaching, already referred to in Part II: the important work of the Council of Europe, and of British linguists on the functional-notional syllabus and English for specific purposes.

The European concern is very much with language as communication, and it adds a further dimension to our conception of language and thus of the role of the teacher. Within this current of development, the learner is seen as a member of society with specific roles to perform in it. This is another kind of learner-centeredness, with many implications for teaching and learning, in which course design springs in the first instance from a needs analysis that is based on sociolinguistic features of communication.

A most striking feature of the current situation is the degree to which it is possible to examine the subject matter to be taught without talking about linguistic form. It is quite apparent that this is what is so intriguing – and at the same time somewhat intimidating – about the communicative approach. The subject matter of the second language classroom has changed from language *forms* to language *use* and language *development*.

Implications for a changed role

A key question in this discussion is thus the determination of exactly what the student or learner acquires in the second language classroom. Does providing for a solid knowledge of language as such still remain the primary responsibility of the language teacher? Perhaps; but it is difficult to sustain the argument that second language teachers teach *only* language structure. Even in the most teacher-centered days, it was always strongly argued that they taught something else. This has always been a characteristic of language teaching that sets it apart from other subjects in a curriculum. During the Grammar-Translation period, the something else was logic and literature; in the postwar period, at least in North America, it was culture, in the anthropological rather than the literary sense. In the contexts in which new languages are taught for daily use by the individuals learning them, a host of other things have been communicated in the classroom along with the second language: how to deal with the local transportation system, good citizenship, how to get along with your neighbors, and so on. Certainly the degree to which teachers are expected to teach or facilitate development of their students' skills in social interaction needs further definition, lest too much be expected from the second language classroom.

All the work in progress in investigating the process of second language development, as well as its product as communicative interaction, points to the need for new classroom strategies. These in turn obviously require a new definition of the role of the teacher, who must be concerned with providing an environment that will supply the appropriate sort of intake and in which the learner can engage in creative interaction. Only then will proper development via strategies that he finds most beneficial take place.

The teacher is no longer director of the process. Nor are teachers the mere instrument of the expert who provides a method to be implemented in the classroom. They are monitor, counselor, consultant, orchestrator, and *animateur*. They will not possess the kind of control as before over the amount, sequencing, and frequency of usage of the items the learners produce or receive. They will work with very different kinds of materials if they are to encourage learners to communicate in order to develop their own language learning – rather than to learn language in order to communicate (Breen, Candlin, and Waters 1979). Furthermore, the subject matter will not be regarded as attached specifically to the study of literature on the one hand, or as completely independent on the other. It will be closely connected to the purposes of the learner and thus to other subjects in the schools if it is taught as part of the school curriculum, or to vocational and professional concerns if it is not.

Attempting a synthesis

There is another way of looking at all of this. Instead of rejecting entirely the earlier models for the teacher, together with everything that has been familiar in second language teaching, it may be possible to synthesize, to come up with a different perspective on what a teacher does. I think that is what will happen. In any case, approaches to education, including second language education, generally tend to be heavily influenced by the expectations of the society that supports them. It is thus difficult to dictate, purely on the evidence from linguistic theory, exactly what the role of the teacher should be. This would lead toward the kind of narrow and rigid definition of second language teaching that the concept of method entailed. In the rest of this work, it will be assumed that teachers are still trying to find their way toward the role that best enables them to carry out their responsibilities, as defined by the teaching context within which they work. It may well be that they will come up with something that is a blend – or they may opt for a pure approach. Whichever route they choose, understanding the theoretical bases of their choice may help them to make a solid and suitable decision.

6 Teachers and linguists

In the preceding chapter, I sketched out an approach to the responsibilities of the language teacher which is suggested by recent changes in the disciplines that contribute to language pedagogy. In this chapter, I would like to explore a little further the zone between linguistics and classroom practice, as well as the relationships among linguists, teachers, and learners. I will also discuss briefly criteria that might assist the teacher to make decisions concerning which of a number of contemporary approaches to take to course design and classroom teaching.

The interplay between the disciplines that constitute the foundations of second language pedagogy on the one hand, and what happens in any given teaching situation on the other, constitutes a swiftly moving field of study. The fundamental disciplines are, of course, theoretical and descriptive linguistics, psycholinguistics, and sociolinguistics. Educational theory as well evidently has to be taken into account where second language teaching goes on in institutional settings. These disciplines interact with classroom practice in different ways and in different proportions, depending on what view is taken of the nature of language, of language learning, and of language teaching.

The linguist dominant

The interaction among the underlying disciplines and classroom practice tended during the 1940s, 50s, and 60s to produce divergent methods of second language teaching. In developing methods, applications of theory to classroom practice were seen as a process of transfer of techniques from descriptive linguistics to teaching, and this resulted in a relationship of linguist to teacher reminiscent of a family tree. Let us take the Audiolingual Method as an example.

In this particular family, linguists like Leonard Bloomfield and Charles Fries played the role of grandfather. Their work was transformed by a second generation of "applied" linguists into teaching materials: *English Pattern Practices* (Lado and Fries 1958) is an obvious example of this process, as are the *Lado English Series* (Lado 1970) and *Modern Spanish* (Bolinger, Ciruti, and Montero 1966). During this time, teachers were trained through the powerful influence of published courses and language laboratory materials, as well as through formal programs. This is nothing new. It should be noted, however, that at the time I am describing, the classroom teacher took training and materials and applied them fairly directly to the conduct of classroom interaction. A well-established pattern for producing second language programs emerged, in which the teacher was a sort of third-generation linguist – or linguist at third remove – faithfully carrying out techniques that had been handed down by a wise forefather.

This view of the methodology of second language teaching, in which it is *derived* from linguistic theory, persists in many models of applied linguistics. One of the best-known of these is Corder's (1973: 156), which although it includes input from socio- and psycholinguistics as well, demonstrates the three-tier conception. Recognition of the need for language policy and planning, and its increasing importance in second language course design, added a fourth source to the process; a current model that incorporates four levels instead of three only is described by Bell. Writing about the European Economic Community's language problems, he refers to the "need to create an integrated language planning process which draws efficiently on existing expertise and represents a collaborative rather than a 'top-down' decision-making process" (Bell 1982: 255). Although this model is collaborative, and although feedback is expected within the systems approach typical of the Council of Europe projects, the classroom teacher appears at the bottom of level 4. This is *after* criteria imposed at political, linguistic, and psychological levels have been met, and after what Bell calls the "professional educationist" has put together contributions from levels 1 to 3 into syllabuses, programs, textbooks, and so on. The teacher is restricted to a how-to-teach role; his output is characterized as "modifications of textbook materials/ personal or group made materials." This appears to be simply a continuation of the family-tree application of linguistics referred to earlier. However, whether to retain this process, and if so, what is to be derived through it, and whether the derivation will produce a standard product, are current issues in second language teaching around the world.

The relationship in question

In fact, the genealogy has changed a great deal. Forefathers have become more numerous as linguistic currents intermingle. Chomsky's dismissal of all empiricist approaches to second language acquisition on the ground that language acquisition is rationalist, and his suggestion that the best that can be done is to provide a linguistically rich environment, have made an enormous impact. Hymes's discussion of communicative competence and his dictum that there are rules of use without which the rules of grammar would be useless (Hymes 1972) have shifted the emphasis from form to communication. Halliday's emphasis on meaning and his work on learning how to mean have further enriched the stock. These contributions, when applied to second language teaching, produced a new legitimacy: teaching for and by communication.

In the context of these changes, questions have already been raised about the validity of trying to retain a linear view of the relationship between linguistics and language teaching. It has, for example, been suggested by Brumfit that it is a mistake to suppose that teaching must be subservient to external disciplines – it has knowledge of its own (Brumfit 1982: 73). An important question becomes whether the classroom teacher is to remain at the end of the line, receiving information from the linguist via the applied linguist, and being expected to apply this information or these insights to the management and conduct of classroom interaction, or whether the teacher–linguist relationship should be redefined.

In response to changes in linguistics, psychology, and education, a number of interesting teaching approaches have arisen which form the bundle now known as "communicative." Communicative teaching exhibits certain distinctive features. It is based on the notion of the learner as communicator, naturally endowed with the ability to learn languages. It seeks to provide opportunities for communication in the classroom as well as to provide learners with the target language system. It is assumed that learners will have to prepare to use the target language (orally and in written form) in many predictable and unpredictable acts of communication which will arise both in classroom interaction and in real-world situations, whether concurrent with language training or subsequent to it.

Although these are features shared by all communicative approaches, it is necessary to distinguish among some contrasting interpretations of how to provide the linguistically rich environment that will lead the learner to communicative competence. These interpretations differ considerably in how they view the relationship between linguist and teacher. They can be arranged on a continuum between an extreme in which the linguist's role is directive and the teacher's dependent (as they have been in the past), and the other in which the linguist's role is descriptive and that of the teacher independent. In this chapter, I want simply to note that the choice of one or another of these approaches has strong implications for what happens in the classroom. I will take the implications for classroom practice of one of the approaches a great deal further in a later chapter.

Five new models

Although there are probably a great many distinctions that could be drawn, I will limit my discussion to five fairly well-developed varieties

61

From theory to practice

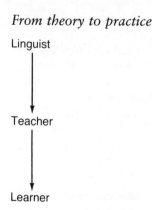

Figure 6.1 Relationships in a functional syllabus.

of communicative language teaching. In addition to the features I have mentioned, they all share a preoccupation with the search for an appropriate methodology. The results are interesting and exciting: The implications for the linguist–teacher relationship are sometimes comfortable, sometimes not so reassuring.

The functional syllabus

The first approach is the provision for functional syllabus specifications (Figure 6.1). To develop such specifications, one requires a description of the desired outcome of instruction in terms of:

– language functions (agreeing, persuading, denying, etc.)
– general as well as specific notions (e.g., "time" – a general notion, and "two o'clock" – a specific notion)
– rhetorical skills (e.g., extracting information from a text, obtaining clarification from a speaker)
– linguistic forms

The canonical approach – if anything as recent as functional language teaching can have such a thing – is to carry out a needs analysis, prepare a set of specifications in the terms I have just described, and leave it to the teachers to use appropriate communicative methodology (e.g., role plays, simulations, information-gap activities, problem-solving activities) in order to get from the syllabus specifications to the desired outcome in student behavior.

The linguist's contribution has been vital in the development of the basis for functional-notional courses. The traditional linear model of transmitting information and making applications of theory underlies the process of developing a functional-notional syllabus and then implementing it. It is true that what is derived is a communicative rather than a structural or formal second language course, but the whole pro-

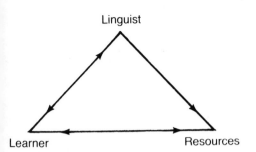

Figure 6.2 Relationships in a negotiated syllabus.

cedure is not dissimilar to the family tree I outlined above. In this case, one might trace the tree as follows: Austin (*How to Do Things with Words, 1962*) to Wilkins (*Notional Syllabuses,* 1976) to, for example, Jones (*Functions of English,* 1977) to the classroom teacher. Teachers can most certainly carry out the procedures involved in building up a functional-notional syllabus, but it took the linguists to get things going in the first place.

The negotiated syllabus

The negotiated syllabus is a variant of the functional syllabus. In this solution, roles are reassigned as follows: The linguist and the learner become the prime actors, and the teacher becomes part of the total instructional resources available. (I should make it clear that I am literally assigning roles for the purposes of discussion; some linguists are, of course, teachers, and some teachers are linguists. There are indeed many learners who are linguists and/or teachers.) The linguist compiles the resources, part of which are in fact the teacher, who exemplifies the target language. Admittedly, this also is not completely new. It goes back to the linguist + native informant of the 1940s (the Army Method; see Carroll 1953). What is derived now, however, is a communicative, not a structural, syllabus. The linguist instructs the learner in the behavior to be expected of a good language learner, and then a process of negotiation concerning the content of each language-learning session takes place.

The relationship is triangular; the interactive relationships are linguist–learner and learner–resources (Figure 6.2). The linguist–resources relationship is unidirectional and the teacher is now a part of those resources – as a facilitator, the partner of the learner, perhaps even an inferior. Of course, the linguist could also perform the role of teacher; I reiterate that though the two activities might be carried out by one person, the *roles* would be differentiated. Here, too, dependence on the linguist is very strong, but the learner is elevated to the level of the

From theory to practice

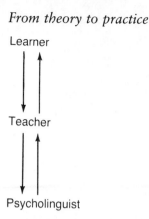

Figure 6.3 Relationships in a natural syllabus.

teacher and interacts directly with the linguist. The linguist–teacher relationship is one in which the linguist retains the directive role, but shares a part of it with the learner once the latter learns how to assume it. Holec discusses this approach under the rubric of self-directed or autonomous learning – freedom from dependence on a teacher, presumably, though not from reliance on the linguist (Holec 1980, 1981). This is the basis for the interactive approach described in Chapter 9.

The natural syllabus

The next of the five varieties is the "natural approach" as it is described by Terrell (1977, 1982). This is an approach based on second language acquisition theory, and the syllabus is assumed to be a natural one, resident in the learner. The most important principle here is that acquisition activities be provided in class. "Experiences" are to be provided in the classroom by a series of affective acquisition activities based on providing comprehensible input, *and* arranged in stages that reflect posited stages of second language acquisition. Presumably in this approach to communication in the classroom, the stages of second language acquisition would be defined by the psycholinguist, and activities proposed by the teacher would be inspected by the psycholinguist to determine whether or not they met linguistically established criteria. This represents a situation of dependence for the teacher, though not of the same kind as in structure-based teaching. Here, the teacher proposes and the linguist disposes, whereas previously it was the linguist who proposed and the teacher who looked after disposal (Figure 6.3).

The subject-matter syllabus

The fourth approach has various forms. It is best known in Canada as immersion teaching (Swain 1978). It is found in both the United States

64

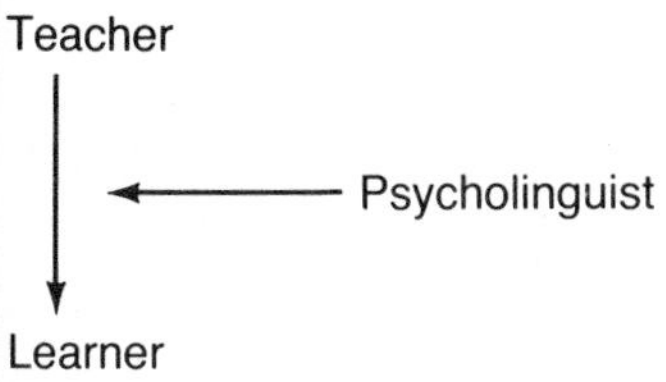

Teacher

|

←——————— Psycholinguist

↓

Learner

Figure 6.4 Relationships in a subject-matter syllabus.

and Canada as the sheltered classroom approach (Wesche 1985). It has other manifestations wherever a subject matter taught through the medium of a target language forms part of the second language learning experience. Quite frequently, it is simply accepted as part of the educational experience, and not labeled explicitly as a second language teaching approach. This would be the case in countries where a language other than the one spoken at home by the students is used as the medium of instruction – for example, English in Nigeria or French in Senegal.

The details differ, but generally a picture of the role of the linguist very different from the traditional one emerges in these immersion or subject-matter approaches (Figure 6.4). The subject-matter teacher takes over and teaches the subject in the usual way, generally with some simplification of language, slowing of pace, and use of gestures to allow for the fact that the learners are not native speakers. Some language instruction is given, though the role of teacher qua language teacher is an ancillary one. The linguist is not required to help design methodology and materials for second language learning, since problems in these areas have to do principally with the provision of interesting and useful learning tasks appropriate to mother tongue teaching. Therefore, the job is one for the subject matter specialist and the psycholinguist: The linguist's role is limited chiefly to making careful observations and measurements as teacher and student get on with the job.[1]

The task-based syllabus

The fifth approach is known as the task-based or procedural syllabus. It is a very new and quite unusual solution (Johnson 1982; Brumfit 1984a). The case in its favor has been put by Prabhu in his discussion of the Bangalore project in India. His central hypothesis is that "structure can best be learned when attention is focused on meaning" (reported in

1 The Modern Language Centre at the Ontario Institute of Studies in Education has recently turned to the investigation of methodology in immersion classes. Fröhlich, Spada, and Allen (1985) report on the development of an instrument for observing the communicative orientation of the second language classroom and suggest that a study which compares instructional differences within a program and relates these differences to proficiency will be carried out – though it is not clear whether in immersion classrooms or not.

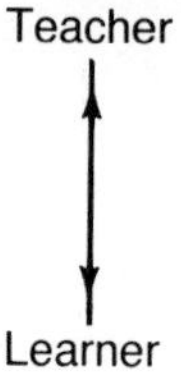

From theory to practice

Teacher

↑
|
|
↓

Learner

Figure 6.5 Relationships in a task-based syllabus.

Johnson 1982). When this becomes the organizing principle for second language teaching programs, the chief focus of classroom work becomes the performance of tasks rather than the language required to perform them. In the Bangalore solution, the tasks include map reading, the interpretation of timetables, solving detective puzzles, and so on. The teacher's task, as far as language is concerned, is to do pretty well what is expected in the third and fourth approaches described earlier: He controls his language so as to provide comprehensible input, as an adult normally does with a child. From Prabhu's description of the project at the TESOL meetings in Honolulu in May 1982, I understood that the tasks were prepared by the teachers alone, on the basis of their own experience and their knowledge of the learners' stage of conceptual development (young children, in this instance), as well as in terms of the reaction they got in the classroom. Johnson (1982: 141) points out that the procedural syllabus may ultimately not escape having linguistic specifications embedded in it (see also Greenwood 1985), but as long as there is little purely linguistic preparation of the learners for the tasks (and I understood that this was the case in Bangalore), this kind of communicative teaching requires very little – if any – direct help from the linguist (Figure 6.5).

Five approaches on a continuum

The five approaches described here represent varying requirements of the linguist's participation. We have seen that in the first approach (the functional-notional syllabus), reliance on the linguist is very heavy. In the negotiated syllabus it is also substantial, but the reliance comes from the learner *as well as from the teacher*. In the natural syllabus, reliance of a different kind is envisaged – that is, on theories of second language acquisition, not on descriptive linguistics. In the fourth approach, the subject-matter syllabus, the linguist's contribution becomes very much less direct. It is certainly possible to imagine explicit teaching of language within the immersion or subject-matter version of communicative language teaching; but this does not mean teaching structure only, since rhetorical organization, appropriateness, register, and so on, would also be considered. Here the linguist would be able to assist by providing descriptions of the target language, including sociolinguistic grammars. Although the methodology for teaching resembles more mother tongue than second language instruction, there is still a linguistic function that can be performed, chiefly to provide insights and to monitor implementation.

Finally, in the fifth model (task-based), the linguist's participation is severely limited. Only if tasks were selected in order to encourage or exercise certain discourse features, such as giving orders, describing processes, and so on, would the linguist play a role. Indeed, a typology of tasks according to discourse features has been proposed by Candlin (1981), and there are such task-based syllabuses in operation. When task-based courses are organized on the basis of such a typology, the linguist is reintroduced into the language learning–language teaching process. If the Bangalore experiment turned out to be convincing and generalizable, however, the linguist would have no role to play in preparing the course materials or syllabus. The interdependence of teacher and learner would be far more important, and the linguist would play a role something like that of the marine biologist watching the medusa and the snail living out their lives in the waters of the Bay of Naples, entirely dependent on each other for survival, and unaware that their interaction is providing occupation for the biologist engaged in observing it.[2]

It seems then that the more emphasis is placed on communicative tasks, the less there will be on the linearity of the relationship of linguist to teacher. If the organizing principles are communicative rather than structural, and the focus of the classroom activity altered from linguistic form to the network of interpersonal meaning, does the linguist become peripheral – even a complete outsider? Not necessarily; it does, however, become necessary to redefine the relationship.

Criteria for choice

My analysis presents a continuum on which several approaches are placed between two extreme visions of the linguist–teacher relationship. At one end the linguist directs the construction of the environment in which second language acquisition is to take place, and provides the resources necessary for the realization of syllabus specifications. The degree of active assistance decreases as one follows the continuum. At the other extreme, the linguist is responsible primarily for monitoring the language learning/language teaching process to see what it reveals

2 This metaphor is inspired by Lewis Thomas's essay "The Medusa and the Snail," in his book of the same name.

about second language acquisition and learning, and the teacher concentrates on developing a stock of exercises for classroom use.

Because there are now a number of alternative approaches to designing second language courses – in addition to simply adopting a structure-based coursebook – there is a pressing need to develop explicit criteria for making decisions about which approach to adopt. It is also necessary to make available more detailed descriptions of these and other approaches, as well as of actual courses based on them. To carry this work forward, it appears that the question "Which is the best model of language teaching?" cannot be answered without the answer to a further question: "What setting is being considered?" Indeed, it would seem difficult at the present time to even talk in terms of a "best" model, without knowing whether resources were available to implement any given model, and without knowing the parameters of a given institutional or noninstitutional setting.

A more productive approach would be to try to match up models of second language teaching with various groups of learners. Some of these matches might be the following:

– Functional syllabuses for beginning ESP learners
– Negotiated syllabuses for sophisticated learners in a language-for-specific-purposes context
– Natural way syllabuses for general education
– Subject-matter syllabuses for general education where rapid progress in the second language was desirable
– Task-based syllabuses for situations where linguistic resources are limited (that is, in a foreign-language teaching context).

Note that these are examples only, and that little empirical evidence is available to suggest that these pairs might be the most effective. Studies of appropriate matchings might very well involve linguists in a specialized role, and would require a good deal of teamwork between teachers and linguists. The characterization of teaching situations, and the preparation of course designs appropriate to each one, would in any case seem to be a more productive route to follow than to turn back to the quest for the perfect single solution. In the next section, I will take this argument a little further, in discussing various ways in which teachers have been involved in course design and in developing appropriate methodology.

7 Teachers and course design

In the preceding chapter, five approaches to second language course design were presented and discussed *in terms of the design of the syllabus*. I want now to turn to methodology as another aspect of course design.

New classroom strategies have been proliferating. Besides the question of how directly linguists can assist teachers, there is now another and more basic problem to be considered: the starting point in course design. There is a large storehouse of teaching techniques to draw from, but how do teachers decide which ones to use and when? Where does one begin and end? All in all, second language teachers can sometimes feel they are faced with a vacuum left by the collapse of the concept of a universal method of instruction. But this is not really the case at all. The problem may be rather that there is so much help at hand that it is difficult to sift through it, and sometimes it is offered somewhat less directly to the practicing teacher than it used to be.

The richest sources of inspiration in course design are now theories of syllabus design on the one hand, and theories of second language development on the other. Far from being incompatible, these two approaches are converging. The meshing of theoretical positions permits the teacher to take into account both psycholinguistic and sociolinguistic theory in planning courses, as well as the inevitable consideration of structural description.

At the same time, there are some issues that are as yet unresolved. One that particularly needs attention is the question of the starting point. When one has a new course to design, when a course needs to be revised or adapted, for whatever reason, should one concentrate on methodology to begin with, and look at classroom techniques as a priority? Or should a syllabus be mapped out in advance? This is a rather basic conflict, especially since there are few prepackaged methods or courses available that can meet everyone's needs. In fact, it appears that teachers will increasingly be called upon to design their own courses. Why this is so has been discussed in the earlier chapters of this work. How to accomplish this and with what resources is the theme of Part IV. Before we can get that far, however, I shall need to explore briefly the relationship between curriculum design and methodology.

Methodology first: the path

There are several versions of the argument for considering methodology first. I shall want to discuss three of them, two of which are related to syllabus types described in the preceding chapter. The third is an approach to language teaching that denies the utility of the syllabus.

Terrell's natural approach

Tracy Terrell is the best-known contemporary proponent of the natural approach to language teaching, although it is by no means his invention. He has acknowledged that he is among those who "rediscovered" it, as it were (see Terrell 1982: fn. 1). What is interesting about Terrell's treatment is that it has assumed a great deal of importance through its link with Krashen's theory of the existence of two separate systems – learning and acquisition – for gaining knowledge about language.[1] Terrell believes that it is quite possible for students to learn to communicate in a classroom situation in a second language, and he does not advocate deferring the goals of communicative competence until advanced levels or special-purpose courses. How to provide for both acquisition *and* learning is thus Terrell's concern, but though his is a communicative approach, he did not initially deal directly with the question of the development of special communicative methodology. Instead he stressed three general principles on which language teaching should be based:

1) the classroom should be devoted primarily to activities which foster acquisition (activities which promote learning might be assigned as homework); 2) the instructor should not correct student speech errors directly; and 3) the students should be allowed to respond in either the target language, their native language, or a mixture of the two. (Terrell 1982: 12)

Of these, he states that (1) is clearly the most important, given the primacy of the acquisition system in Krashen's theory.

Terrell's emphasis, like Krashen's, is clearly on the process of language acquisition rather than on the product, and from Krashen's research it is possible to derive pedagogical principles similar to Terrell's.[2] However, Krashen in his early work appeared not just to ignore but to view as irrelevant many factors that had previously been considered essential in second language course design. He seemed to take for granted that since there is a natural process of second language acquisition – or a natural

---

1 Terrell discusses Krashen's theory and its implications for his own work at some length in Terrell (1982). See also Krashen (1981, 1982).
2 Krashen and Terrell (1983) further clarify the relationship of Krashen's theory to Terrell's approach.

syllabus that will in any case emerge – there is no need to design an artificial progression for the learner. One has only to provide conditions in which learners can develop communicative competence in their own way and in their own time.

Terrell has translated this attitude into a statement on methodology (Terrell 1982: 129). He suggests a developmental progression, from receptive to productive skill, using (in the order cited) Asher's technique of Total Physical Response (Asher 1977), question-and-answer drills, dialogues, and finally various strategies designed to encourage problem solving and interaction in the classroom.

Until the appearance of *The Natural Approach* (Krashen and Terrell 1983), Krashen had not been primarily concerned with methodology, although he certainly had expressed his views on classroom procedures. "The major function of the second language classroom," he wrote, "is to provide intake for acquisition. . . . one could also say that the major challenge facing the field of applied linguistics is to create materials and contexts that provide intake" (Krashen 1981: 101). Intake does not have a syllabus that can be created by the linguist or anyone else. It appears of its own accord, and both linguist and teacher must be alive to its presence. It is not, however, their creation. Their role, in such a context, is quite different from that of the linguist or teacher who *imposes* a structure for the acquisition of linguistic forms. Yet there is a linguistic syllabus, which has to be reflected in the methodology used.

The implications of this approach to course design are still being worked out. It is, however, clear that the relationship between the "shape of the curriculum" (Savignon 1983: 187) and the syllabus that learners bring with them is not clear. The syllabus is presented in terms of the methodology to be used in the classroom, that is, in terms of classroom techniques (such as those referred to earlier: question-and-answer drills, problem solving, etc.) arranged in a specific sequence. But what of the linguistic content of the classroom activities? Who determines this? On what basis? As soon as already existing published materials are used, for example, the danger of falling back on a structural approach exists. Thus, although the argument is for a natural syllabus, in practice it may be a linguistic one being employed.

Immersion teaching

Another variant of the "methodology first" school of thought is clearly embodied in the immersion model of bilingual education. It continues to grow in popularity and strength in Canada and elsewhere, and it is being adapted for adult learners. Here also methodology is used that is not at all similar to what was regarded until recently as appropriate to the second language classroom. Stern described the basic philosophy of immersion in these terms:

> In order to learn a language, it is important that learners from a very early stage of language learning become involved in real-life communication. . . . The most accessible form of 'real life' is the school situation itself, and by offering part of the school curriculum or even the whole curriculum in the second language, the learner is immersed into a communicative setting in which the second language is used naturally. (Stern 1980: 57–8)

Thus the matter of methodology is treated in a manner similar to Krashen's: Caretaker speech is provided, and the focus is on communication about real-life matters. The question of curriculum (or syllabus) design is taken care of, not in terms of linguistic content but of other regular school subjects and *their* syllabuses.[3] Language is directly related to other classroom activities, and comes out of them. The learner has to concentrate on acquiring not language, but "techniques for language acquisition," or what Stern has called "coping techniques" (Stern 1981).[4] Systematic teaching of language arts is included along with the teaching of subject matter in immersion teaching, but the approach used involves developing both languages *as though each were a mother tongue* (see Bibeau 1982). Since the aim of these programs is to produce students with functional competence in the second language, as well as to maintain and develop normal levels of first language competence, certain concessions are made to the fact that the second language is in fact not a mother tongue.

In a recent review of the literature on immersion experiments, Genesee characterizes immersion by the following pedagogical conditions:

1. The students are permitted to use their home language in school and in the classroom at least during the initial part of the program. The students continue to use their home language amongst themselves at all stages of the program.
2. Attempts by the students to use the second language for communicative purposes are strongly encouraged by the teachers or conversely, grammatical or structural errors in the students' communicative use of the second language are not given undue attention.

---

3 The distinction between syllabus and curriculum is worth repeating (see Chapter 3): *Syllabus* means the specification of content for a single course or subject, and *curriculum* refers to the collectivity of course offerings at an educational institution (or group of institutions).

4 See also Savignon (1972). Savignon discusses the need for techniques to encourage students to develop information-getting skills, in order to involve them in real-life communicative experiences from the very beginning of their study of a second language. In fact, these "coping techniques" were at the very heart of her study, which describes one of the first experiments in communicative language teaching.

3. Both the first and second languages are used for regular curriculum instruction in addition to language arts instruction.

$\qquad\qquad$ (Genesee 1983: 3)

He also mentions that the teachers act as monolingual models, although
they understand both languages. Immersion teaching has been adapted
by researchers and teachers of second languages at the University of
Ottawa, with considerable success (Wesche 1985). It appears to be applicable, with variation at the level of nonlinguistic content, to every
possible age group.

I have included the lengthy quotation from Genesee because his basic
pedagogical conditions for immersion teaching, taken together with
Stern's, resemble quite closely Terrell's general principles. One might
say that this approach departs even further from any semblance of linguistic syllabus – at least, from any linguistic syllabus that might be
appropriate for second language teaching. It resembles mother tongue
teaching, in which knowledge of the language forms is assumed to a
certain extent. In this regard, it is based on a nativist theory of language
learning or acquisition, and falls into the group of teaching approaches
in which the emphasis is on meaning, and not on form.

Teaching language as communication

The two preceding approaches are naturalistic versions of communicative language teaching, in which methodology is of more interest than
syllabus design. If the latter is present at all, it is not in the form of the
traditional linguistic syllabus, but as either (a) an inborn, unavoidable
sequence of acquisition of the linguistic forms of the target language, or
(b) an inborn ability to acquire the linguistic forms of the target language
as though it were a first language. The distinction is real enough; and
the methodologies used are distinct as well.

There is also a third and even stronger version of the argument for
developing a methodology designed to foster communicative competence
rather than worrying about syllabus design. It has been suggested that
many teachers, seeing their main purpose now as enabling learners to
become communicatively proficient, require new kinds of language
teaching materials (Candlin and Breen 1979; Breen and Candlin 1980).
Using these materials, learners will be encouraged to apply their natural
abilities of interpretation, expression, and negotiation – the last being
the central or pivotal activity in performing all communicative acts.

In seeking to develop a suitable classroom context within which these
abilities will develop in the second language, this approach explicitly
rejects the need to have a syllabus on hand before implementing a second
language course. It is quite possible to systematize language teaching

materials if the teacher is presenting language as form, but it is not possible if language is being taught as communication – which by nature is unpredictable, unsystematizable.

Although this is an argument based upon a theory of the nature of language as communication (a linguistic theory), rather than on a theory of how we acquire it (a psycholinguistic theory), it leads to conclusions that are similar to the arguments outlined previously – namely, that teachers and course designers ought to be much more concerned with the *ways* learners may act upon and interact with linguistic data than with the prior selection and organization of the data. This is certainly an approach that fits in with the general principles of communicative language teaching outlined earlier in this work. Indeed, it elevates the concept of learner centeredness to new heights, since it advocates focusing not only on learners' interests but on their capacities for data selection and organization. Thus, in this very strong version of the methodology argument, the primary consideration is for materials; the need for an organizing frame of reference is of a different order of importance.

The syllabus first: the goal

The preceding section was intended to develop further the description of communicative approaches to course design. Three versions have been discussed, ranging from the "natural way," which on close inspection is the one that most nearly resembles traditional second language courses, to the immersion approach and the "language-as-communication" approaches, which are respectively further from that model.

In Chapter 1, variations on the traditional linguistic syllabus were presented, and in Chapter 6 five contemporary approaches to syllabus design were discussed. In some of these communicative approaches to course design, the element of syllabus is relegated to second place in setting up second language teaching programs. The salient characteristic of all three approaches is that they are all process-oriented. All come via different paths to similar conclusions about language teaching: that the teacher's concern should be primarily with the route, not the goal – with what Richterich has called the "learner's trajectory" (Richterich et al. 1981). Along the way, procedures of linguistic syllabus design are considered marginally important if not irrelevant.

From the perspective of language course planning, though the trajectory is important, one cannot ignore the goal. At least for now, society expects teachers to be able to describe and justify objectives in terms of language behavior at the point of exit from a course or courses. Teachers are accountable; learners want to know where they are going. The problem thus becomes to accommodate both concerns: on the one hand, concern for appropriate and effective classroom interaction, and on the other, for a satisfactory outcome given the time and facilities available. Concern with methodology as well as with syllabus design can help in this task.

A synthesis

How may a synthesis be accomplished? Let us consider anew the three arguments for permitting the natural growth of language to take place in the classroom. Of the three, I find the arguments for immersion or subject-matter teaching to conflict least with the need for some planning in the form of a syllabus. To begin with, though in the early forms of immersion teaching there was no linguistic syllabus as such, there was a conceptual scheme and a support for language activities provided by the syllabus for regular subjects. The balance between emphasis on language study and emphasis on functional use of language had been righted, since for young children the use of language to negotiate meaning is clearly more important than its formal study. A shift back to the inclusion of some language study is now perceived as desirable in immersion teaching; it represents a new redressing of the balance between language development and language use, a sort of fine tuning of the immersion model. In any case, a plan of study is mapped out before classroom interaction begins.

The "nature of language as communication" arguments leave less room for prior design of a syllabus. Candlin has suggested that "syllabuses place a premium on the specification of content" and that this often occurs without reference to classroom actualization of the syllabus (Candlin 1984: 31). As a solution to this problem, he proposes replacement of all models which produce the kind of syllabus that "transmits preselected and often predigested knowledge" by one that "is social and problem-solving in its orientation," and in which "participants, both teachers and learners, are encouraged to ask questions from the outset about syllabus objectives, content, methodology and experiences, and their evaluation" (Candlin 1984: 34). Evidently, in using such a model, the outcomes would be unpredictable because they would be unpremeditated, and long-term planning would be impossible, even harmful.

Candlin has, however, recently suggested a two-stage approach to planning at what he calls the curriculum and syllabus levels (Candlin 1984: 35). This would meet the requirements for institutional planning at least, and would bring this argument closer into line with the two-phase approach to preparing courses whose objective is communicative proficiency (see Chapter 9). Thus there seems to be an opening to accommodation of Candlin's arguments within the model I will propose below.

75

Terrell and Krashen's natural approach is the most difficult to rec-
oncile with any interest in syllabus design based on language learning
or language use. For it is an approach rooted in the distinction made
by Krashen between learning and acquisition, and based on a posited
developmental progression. Krashen's learning–acquisition hypothesis
is still being debated, and there is opposition to it, based on several
grounds: it cannot be proved either true or false; it is basically meta-
physical; his data can be interpreted according to hypotheses other than
those he advances; he uses such terms as "conscious" and "subconscious" in a sense that is not usual, but that he does not define (see, e.g.,
Sharwood-Smith 1981; Bibeau 1983; Brumfit 1984b; Gregg 1984).

I shall limit my own contribution to the simple statement that, though
Krashen's work is a brilliant synthesis of the research in second language
learning and teaching, I cannot accept his categorical distinction between
learning and acquisition or his theory that they represent distinct and
independent ways of developing competence in a second language. Instead, I believe that they must be viewed as elements in a single process
of language development. Likewise, I would have no quarrel with Terrell's pedagogical principles, as long as they are not interpreted to mean
that learning activities must be excluded from the classroom. A good
deal of time spent on communicative activities may well be desirable –
but some balance between language study as such and functional use
needs to be maintained in order to arrive at optimal development of
both fluency and accuracy in a second language. (The fluency–accuracy
distinction has been described by Brumfit in various publications, especially Brumfit 1980, 1984b.)

Later on, I shall turn to the question of exactly what form the linguistic
component of a syllabus might take. For the moment I want merely to
observe that this component need not necessarily be excluded from
communicatively oriented courses. If Terrell's and Candlin's writings are
closely examined, it will be apparent that neither banishes metalinguistic
study totally from the classroom; and the immersion model does include
language arts, as I noted earlier. The principal problem is to develop
models of course design that provide the correct balance among all
possible elements, in view of the needs of specific target groups of
learners.

In planning second language programs today, theory from both
schools of thought should be applied. Three major contributions come
from the methodologists:

– general principles governing classroom interaction
– access to the use of authentic samples of language through work in
  discourse analysis
– a wide range of suitable methodology

Suitable methodology, using authentic language texts, includes:

- hidden ways of handling structures (such as Terrell describes)
- teaching through the target language, that is, using the target language as the medium of instruction
- all the "communicative" techniques, ranging from simulations, games, and role plays (the initial response to the methodology issue) to newer techniques and materials that involve problem-solving and inferencing abilities.

Theories of syllabus design assist the construction of frameworks (see p. 80) for the content of second language courses. These permit the generalization and incorporation into the course design of learners' needs, wants, and desires. Those language functions and notions that are most important can serve as springboards for necessary language forms, and these in turn will be treated or exercised through materials and techniques made available by those working in the area of materials design. The specification of content for a course will serve to identify areas of interest to learners, and about which they need to be able to express themselves.

Constraints in syllabus design

By designing a syllabus – that is to say, limiting the content of a course – I do not mean limiting the language to be used so as to produce a linguistic robot. Since time is a constraint in all second language teaching situations, it is necessary to pay attention to problems of management. The limitations of the teachers themselves often constrain course design as well. How then is one to cope with defining content and setting standards, as well as with classroom interaction? A syllabus is an instrument to be used to coordinate all these aspects of language teaching. As such, it should not be rigid, but flexible; not closed, but open-ended; and not static, but subject to constant revision as a result of feedback from the classroom.

In view of the existence of two rather different points of view regarding the starting point in course design (methodology and syllabus specification), there is a need to look further for some organizing principles that can provide a conceptual scheme within which the findings on linguistic and psycholinguistic research can be accommodated. This conceptual scheme will also need to permit some planning of classroom management consistent with general educational theory and the present sociocultural contexts in which second language teaching takes place.

Two phases in course design

One way of coping with this problem is to divide the work involved in designing a second language course into two phases. The first phase is what is thought of as classic syllabus design: the preparation of syllabus specifications, comprising a greater or lesser number of components, *as theory and practice dictate* (see the discussion of proficiency in Chapter 2). This is the stage at which one might first obtain data on the learners as well as on the physical constraints present in the teaching situation, and, second, ask oneself in how many categories information is available – and if available, useful. Finally, one might produce a description of the language teaching situation – its learners, goals, and classroom environment – as well as one of the target language situations, as far as these are known.

The second phase of the design process consists in exploiting the information thus collected so that communication and interaction may take place in the classroom. This is the phase of development that is least elaborated in communicatively oriented approaches to language teaching, and in which consequently there is much work to be done. In curriculum guides for second language teaching, one often finds excellent charts for the presentation of structures, comprehensive lists of language forms, as well as generalizations or concepts, and vocabulary topics. Together with these specifications, there may be a section on teaching techniques. All of this constitutes the first stage of syllabus design. Even with all this material available, however, the teacher still needs to work it into units of some sort, since it is far from classroom-ready.[5]

It is at this point that the concept of the pedagogical syllabus, or pedagogical handbook, becomes useful. For each course designed from a set of specifications (e.g., *Threshold Level English, French Core Programs* 1980, or any set produced to meet local needs), a handbook may be prepared. The basic unit of organization might be a thematic one, or it might be one or other of the communicative functions of language. There are many possibilities for organization, which is why one should consider the matter of a syllabus *type* before entering this phase of the design.

Several of these syllabus types have now been proposed for use in implementing communicative language programs, in ESL and in other languages. (Discussion of possible models began in Alexander 1975 and has continued in Müller 1980; Johnson 1982; and Yalden 1983.) Here are some of the proposed solutions:

– A model in which functional teaching is grafted onto a structural core (Brumfit 1980).
– The variable-focus model, which involves changing emphasis or focus

5 *Threshold Level English* (van Ek 1980), of course, contains all these specifications except for teaching techniques. *French Core Programs* (1980) is an example of a document that contains techniques as well as all the rest. These publications and others like them cannot, however, be used for *immediate preparation of* classroom-ready materials.

from one aspect of language to another as time progresses (Allen 1980).

- The proportional model, in which topics or specific notions are used as a framework for a gradual change of proportion in the time devoted to language form on the one hand and communicative function and discourse structure on the other – or vice versa, depending on the underlying theory of second language learning (Yalden 1983).
- The entirely functional models used in English for science and technology and English for academic purposes, designed for learners who have to carry out predictable roles. An EST example might be air traffic controllers; an EAP group could be students of petrochemical engineering. In these models, teaching tasks mirror objectives.
- The procedural model (Johnson 1982: 135–44; Brumfit 1984a; Beretta and Davies 1985), in which tasks are designed to produce general language competence.
- Another task-based model, in which tasks are designed to foster strategies for learning and communication (Candlin and Breen 1979).
- A process-oriented model, in which "a predesigned content syllabus would be publicly analysed and evaluated by the classroom group, or an emerging content syllabus would be designed (and similarly evaluated) in an on-going way" (Breen 1984: 55).
- The model in which some other subject matter provides a nonlinguistic syllabus, as in sheltered courses and in immersion programs.

A large range of possibilities. There are no doubt more to come. How does one decide which to incorporate into the design for a given program?

Reprise: criteria for selection

Criteria appear from outside the teaching context, as well as from within it. For example, many of the criteria that have to be applied in selecting one or another model (or in creating new ones) come from the area of language policy. Government policy frequently has a profound effect on what language is taught to whom and for what purpose. It also clearly affects financing. Thus, one might have to adopt a functional model if time were short and the teaching institution bound by contract to deliver certain services. On the other hand, although language policy will affect the amount of time available for language teaching in the schools, such teaching is often stretched out over a number of years. In such a case, either the proportional or the variable-focus model might be appropriate.

The age, educational background, and the expectations of learners will also constrain choice of syllabus type. Not all learners will accept new types of classroom activities, but others can quickly adapt to communicatively oriented ones, even if they have been used to structure-based drills only.

Theoretical criteria are naturally of great importance. Those responsible for planning second language teaching programs will try as much as possible to adopt procedures consistent with the theories of second language learning and teaching to which they subscribe. That is obvious. What would be helpful, however, is some empirical research oriented toward comparing second language course designs, with a view to formulating a position on what types of curriculum work best in which circumstances.

Segmenting the curriculum

One possible avenue is to divide a course or program into segments of varying lengths, each of which is conducted according to a different orientation or design. It would be possible, for example, to begin an ESL program for foreign students in a university setting with a short structural segment, if their knowledge of English were at a low level. One might continue with a longer segment designed along proportional lines (see Figure 9.3, p. 96). A concluding segment would then be designed along the lines of a classic ESP program (Robinson 1980) and could be given concurrently with courses in the learners' academic discipline. I do not claim that this is necessarily the best design. I only wish to point out that it is possible to join together segments of different kinds within an overall program. It will take more experimentation to arrive at the right degree of adjustment for each course, but syllabus design now permits this. It is quite feasible to change the proportions without necessarily committing teachers to a single methodology for the duration of the whole program. In other words, the segmented syllabus offers a pragmatic solution until further theoretical advances are made, and may well help in achieving new insights.

Frameworks for course design

In the second phase of the design process, once the basic form of the syllabus has been decided upon, there are various ways to prepare the curriculum. One, based on the proportional model, consists in setting objectives for units of work in terms of topics and communicative and rhetorical functions. A choice of appropriate classroom techniques and tasks that exploit relevant language samples is decided on. Important or necessary language forms are chosen as well.

Then it is up to the teacher, ideally with the aid of the learner or learners, to negotiate which activities are to be used on a given day during a given lesson. By varying activities, the same unit based on topics and functions can be used cyclically on several occasions. By so doing, the range of language forms and items associated with a given topic and functions can be extended considerably.

If units are prepared in this way, a great variety of courses can be produced from them, in which there is room for a large number of teaching techniques. From a set of basic units that constitute a framework, several teachers might produce several different classroom plans. These frameworks offer the possibility of maximum flexibility at a time when much still remains to be accomplished in needs analysis, in discourse analysis, in the study of communicative competence and its components, and in the study of second language learning. They also offer the control required to permit further evaluation of teaching techniques of all kinds. To use a horticultural image, they might be regarded as trellises provided in order to support a young plant as it develops to maturity. Once it does, the trellis is obscured by the density and complexity of the growth, and only the plant can be seen.

Part IV *Frameworks for second language course design*

At the end of Part III, I introduced the notion of a single framework from which a whole range of *different* second language courses could be produced (see also Yalden 1983: 149). It is time now to examine this idea in greater detail, and to see how it may be applied to a variety of teaching contexts.

It should be clear that, in the present work, the notion of a single language teaching method, applicable to all educational contexts, and to all groups of learners, has been rejected. It should be equally clear that this does not mean that the preparation of a second language course can be approached in a totally cavalier fashion, with the intention to do whatever occurs to the teacher or learner on the spur of the moment. Every teacher, moreover, proceeds from a theoretical base, no matter how inexplicit or unconscious it may be. And all learners want to have some idea of what they are expected to learn. There are, then, several requirements for organizing the methodology that is going to be used.

Where is one to turn for the principles of organization, if the notion of method is rejected? If there is an alternative, why should it be useful, when there are so many methods already in use?

The answer to the first question is that work in syllabus and curriculum design can provide alternatives to method. As to the second, I shall try to provide an answer in the remaining chapters. To illustrate the *frameworks approach*, several projects carried out at the Centre for Applied Language Studies at Carleton University, Ottawa, are described. Each involved different kinds of constraints on teaching, and different kinds of learners. Accordingly, different frameworks were prepared for each context, from which teachers and learners together elaborated their own courses, according to their own needs and preferences. The results have been encouraging, and can now be applied to a variety of other teaching situations, in which the frameworks will assist teachers to prepare courses to suit local conditions.

The question of methodology will not be overlooked; it is an integral part of course design, and has to be carefully considered. What one hopes for in using the frameworks is a balanced approach to the question of which comes first, syllabus or methodology. Why not consider them together – and get some help from learners who are to be chiefly affected by the decisions taken and the choices made during the preparatory phases of second language course design?

As theoretical work in curriculum building for language teaching advances, the idea of a step that lies between the preparation of linguistic material to be taught and the classroom seems to be taking root. As we have seen (Chapter 1), the preparation of a pedagogical grammar was considered for quite some time to precede classroom work *directly*. That is, the description of a language, based on a particular theory of grammar, usually traditional or structuralist, was interpreted for language teaching purposes. What was produced was a pedagogical grammar: "an interpretation and selection for language teaching purposes of the description of a language, based not only on linguistic, but also on psychological and educational criteria" (Stern 1983: 186).

Many observers (e.g., Stern 1983: esp. chap. 9) now feel that a pedagogical grammar alone is insufficient in itself as the curriculum for a second language course. Stern suggests that a corresponding *sociolinguistic* guide may be prepared, to be used apart from, or together with, the linguistic one. If they are combined they might be called a *pedagogical language guide* (Stern 1983: 187). This is in fact fairly close to my notion of *frameworks*. In his discussion of the interaction between linguistics and language teaching, Stern describes a three-level relationship, in which the first is the level of theoretical linguistics, the second, that of the pedagogical grammar, and the third, that of the second language curriculum or language syllabus and of materials development.

In any case, other aspects of communicative competence need to be developed, and to this end, a richer curriculum is required. In the following chapters, I shall give further consideration to working out course designs that will help develop the components of second language competence.

8 Syllabus and methodology

It is difficult, in considering course design, to separate the issues found in general language programs from those that arise in specific-purposes courses. There are more similarities than one might suppose. The relationship of the syllabus designer may be to a sponsor or employer, or it may be to parents and educational institutions. In each case, however, decisions will be taken by the former that will have a steering effect on teacher–learner interaction. This is true whether the designer of the course is the classroom teacher or not.

Questions of accountability are also present in both settings. As long as accountability of the teacher to the student, or of the educational institution to the client, is a consideration, the syllabus for a second language program is not a guide for private use by the teacher. It is a record. It concerns, in the first instance, the object of the instruction, its social purpose. The means also have to be negotiated; but this is a secondary consideration, for in all negotiation, many constraints other than those dictated by the physical setting of instruction and the current state of pedagogical theory must be considered. For example, constraints imposed by language planning also have to be considered, since the time available, resources, and motivational factors may all be dependent on the status of the target language. The age of the learners and content of instruction can obviously be affected as well (Bell 1982). In some cases, one can go even further: Judd states that teaching English to speakers of other languages is "a political act. . . . Those of us engaged in teaching of English to non- or limited-English speakers are . . . directly or indirectly, implementing a stated or implied language policy" (Judd 1984). All the more reason to work out a statement about the goals of instruction and the means to be used in reaching them.

The need for a planning instrument of some kind is clear. Much of the contemporary debate centers on various methods of language instruction, most of which are now seen as dealing primarily with the structural or linguistic component of second language learning. With the advent of more complex theories of language and language learning, as well as a recognition of the diversity of learners' needs, wants, and aspirations, the concept of the syllabus for second language teaching has taken on new importance and has become more elaborate. As a result, it has been examined at length, particularly in the context of English

85

for specific purposes programs, but also more and more in general planning for language teaching.[1] It thus replaces the concept of method. The syllabus is now seen as an instrument by which the teacher, with the help of the syllabus designer, can achieve a certain coincidence between the needs and aims of the learner, and the activities that will take place in the classroom. It is thus a necessity in terms of providing educational services to the community to which the teacher is responsible.

Efficiency

A syllabus enhances efficiency in two ways. The first is a matter of *pragmatic efficiency* or economy of time and money. The setting of instruction has to be planned. Not all learners will be given the same treatment, and syllabuses differ according to the practical constraints present in any given situation. The second point of interest is *pedagogical efficiency:* economy in the management of the learning process. Instruction provided in an institutional setting is assumed to be a more efficient method than allowing the learner to proceed in a nonstructured environment. This has long been recognized, even though individuals have always also managed to acquire second language proficiency independently. Even the most ardent supporters of the natural growth school will admit that classroom instruction is both desirable and necessary (cf. Allen 1984: 65–7).

Thus, it is clear that a syllabus of any kind is viewed as providing for control of the learning process (Widdowson 1984) and that this is necessary to attain an efficient approach to second language teaching and learning. Generally, the control is exercised by the institution or the teacher, but in some instances control can and should also be exercised by the learner. Although the term "syllabus" may have negative connotations in the literature of education,[2] it is used here in a particular sense that must be made clear. The degree and type of control that the syllabus exercises depends on the institution: In certain institutions, it will be determined by consensus rather than imposed. In others, it will be decreed and will have to be followed. The point to be recognized is that if it is to be arrived at by discussion and mutual understanding, there is another aspect of its design to be considered, together with efficiency.

1 See for example the *Programmes d'études, anglais et français langues secondes,* prepared by the Ministry of Education of the Government of Quebec.
2 This has been the case in Ontario, where local school boards have a great deal of autonomy, and full syllabuses are not provided by the Ministry of Education.

Explicitness

A syllabus for language teaching must of course be explicit for the teacher, and should be at least partially produced by teachers. In fact it often is produced entirely by teachers. Help from experts of various kinds is often not available or not needed. The relationship of the syllabus designer to the teacher can range along the continuum described in Chapter 6. One thing is certain, however: To have the teacher participate in syllabus production ensures complete understanding of the end product. The need for economy in planning and in teacher preparation is thus very well served whenever the teacher acts as course designer, whether alone or with help.

A syllabus can also be more or less explicit for the learner. The learner must have some idea of content, but the extent to which learners help to determine either ends or means depends on their educational background, age, type of second language program, and a host of other factors. The point is that learner participation in course design should not be excluded *a priori,* whatever the setting, including that of courses for young children.

A final important observation: A syllabus must be seen as making explicit what will be taught, not necessarily what will be learned. A range of outcomes must be expected. The expression of objectives for a course does not have to constitute an expression of objectives for a *given* group of learners. It is better viewed as a summary of the content to which learners will be exposed. Any adaptation or realization of a set of specifications for a syllabus may include objectives, to be sure; but they should be expressed in terms of a range, and students' achievements should also be expected to fall within an acceptable range rather than being narrowly defined.

Organizing principles

Since a syllabus includes many practical and social constraints, it is only partly answerable to principles determined by theories of language and of second language learning. Other organizing principles related, for example, to overall curriculum design, and the prevailing philosophy of education, must also enter into play. This is a common state of affairs (see, e.g., Brumfit 1980). Let us set them aside for the moment, however, and consider only general principles directly connected with the development of a syllabus for language.

A syllabus should be, in the first instance, a statement about content, and only in a later stage of development a statement about methodology

87

and materials to be used in a particular teaching context. The need for efficiency dictates the need for organization of content but may also affect the organization of materials. In any discussion of organizing principles, it is generally assumed that both sequencing and continuity of content should be considered.

In recent years, in view of the inclusion of sociolinguistic and discourse competence (as well as grammatical competence) in the target definitions of second language proficiency, there has been much discussion of how to identify types of meaning and thus the components of communicative competence. This has in turn led to concern over which elements of language can be taught systematically and which nonsystematically, what can be approached in a linear fashion and what cyclically (Johnson 1980). Answers to these questions depend on one's view of language as a part of the sum of human knowledge, of how and how much of this knowledge can be transmitted, and of what the conditions for such transmission may be.

The options

Taking into account the present state of linguistic theory, statements about organizing principles for a language syllabus can be reduced to a set of options. The principles might be answerable to one of the three following views of language:

– how it is learned (largely, but not only, via conscious strategies)
– how it is acquired (only via subconscious processes)
– how it is used.

Let us consider each of these possibilities in turn. If learning is taken as a first principle, it follows that organization based on the structural core should be chosen, on the grounds that "we are more likely to learn effectively what can be perceived as a system than what can only be perceived as unrelated items" (Brumfit 1981: 91).[3] That is, it appears that structure is the only aspect or component of language that can be taught systematically, and it follows therefore that it should form the backbone of instruction.

3 It has been suggested to me (Peter Strevens, personal communication) that Brumfit meant here that schemata are better learned than discrete items. It is quite possible that Brumfit was thinking of the integration of a preexisting system (the grammar of the target language) into another system (the learner's schema) in writing the article referred to. However, it seems to me that the citation I give refers to internal organization of a syllabus, rather than to the cognitive mechanisms for organization of data in the learner. I interpret his remarks as referring to the likelihood of learning the system of grammar as being easier (because it is perceived as a system) than learning functions or notions that may appear as a collection of disparate elements to the learner. He suggests that if a syllabus is based upon such units, they have to be given a semblance of coherence through the use, for example, of a story line.

If acquisition is taken as a first principle, then linguistic content for a syllabus does not need to be heavily organized. Instead, the right environment for the natural growth of the target language should be provided. This probably implies some study of the interests and characteristics of the learner, in order to provide nonlinguistic content to the syllabus. But no strictly linguistic criteria (of surface morphological or syntactic complexity, for example) need be applied in selection and sequencing. Psycholinguistic and motivational criteria are to be preferred, for the organizing principle is the theory of natural language development. One of the axioms of this theory is that language development occurs in a series of stages, which can be described empirically. Classroom activities (whatever their content) should thus be graded according to these stages (Terrell 1977, 1982; Krashen 1982).

If language use is taken as the first principle, we would have to agree with Wilkins (1981) that no particular organizing principle emerges, and one may take different things on different occasions as starting points. Yet whatever aspect of language is chosen as a starting point, the others must also receive attention. It is assumed that a forecast of the settings for use of the target language will be available, and that it will considerably influence the design of the course. This in turn implies the presence of a needs analysis.

It is this third type of organization that seems to present the most fruitful possibilities for contributions to course design from the learner. Without rejecting the other types of organization, I want to present in what follows an argument in favor of adopting the principle of language use as the primary one in second language course design.

Language use

No matter what the context, there is general agreement that the provision of a useful and stimulating approach to second language learning is desirable. Thus it would be as well to accomplish two related tasks in course design:

– to stress the connections between present study and future use
– to exploit the "inter-organism" more fully than the "intra-organism" aspects of second language development in the classroom (Halliday 1978; see also Ellis 1981, 1984).

In order to attain the first objective, to link language study to future use, some information on the purposes for which the target language will be used can be of great value – even in general education. Adoption of the principle of language use as the chief one in course design can be instrumental in meeting one of the major difficulties in second language teaching: that is, how to provide the content around which communi-

89

cative interaction in the classroom can take place, when there is no longer a standard method to be followed. Some idea of the components of a classical syllabus design (and how to get information on or from a particular group of learners) does indeed help to provide ideas for the ideational content of a course.

This procedure leads naturally and logically to the second task: concentration on the inter-organism aspects of second language development in the classroom. This kind of emphasis does not exclude consideration of and experimentation with the natural growth sequences that may exist. It is rather a matter of emphasis in syllabus design. The inter-organism emphasis also accommodates concern with language as communication. Since all language learners have communicative abilities that they share with all other users of the target language, classroom activities should be geared to having them exercise these natural abilities. However, in order to spark communication in the classroom, or anywhere else, one must have something to communicate about, and needs analysis procedures can contribute greatly to determining what topics might be of interest.

Conclusion

If we go back to a consideration of the principles of learning and of acquisition vis-à-vis language use, we will find that they can be viewed as applicable at different times in course design. If one focuses, in the first phase of the course design process, on language use, then during the second phase – materials and methodology – one can very well consider principles of learning and acquisition. One need not exclude the other. Concern with learning and acquisition is concern with structural and psychological aspects of the language system. Concern with language use gives other aspects equal or greater weight.

In most analyses of communicative competence being used today in preparing second language programs, many components other than the purely linguistic are included. Psycholinguistic considerations are obviously very important. Until recently, however, sociolinguistic concerns have tended to be neglected, or not sufficiently developed. Brumfit (1984b) suggests that the syllabus has linguistic, interactional, and content aspects; Ullmann (1982) describes a model for syllabus design that includes separate components for language, communicative activity, culture, and general language education. In order to include such components of language and communication, and to provide opportunities for language development in each area, we must greatly expand the complexity of syllabus design. In so doing, the linguistic component loses its predominant position, and the design for language learning takes on a different shape from the one that most teachers are familiar with. In the next chapter, I shall turn to the description of a specific kind of structure for a syllabus based on the principle of language use.

9 A proportional approach

Throughout what follows, it is assumed that the principle of language use is fundamental in course design for second language teaching. The inter-organism aspects of second language development in the classroom should be stressed and exploited from the start of syllabus design. In this phase (preparing the "protosyllabus") the design process is focused on settings in which the second language might be used, as well as topics and themes that are likely to arise (whether job-related or connected to learners' personal interests and inclinations). In the *second* phase (designing and implementing the pedagogical syllabus) intra-organism concerns can be taken into account. At this level, psychological factors need to be considered and activities chosen that will accommodate the learning style of the individuals concerned and thus facilitate learning. General methodological principles will be determined, then specific teaching techniques can be slotted in to provide the desired emphasis on various aspects of the learners' developing competence.

To clarify this separation of the course design process into several phases, I shall discuss briefly the model of language program design and a particular type of syllabus design, both of which I have treated more extensively in earlier works (Yalden 1983, 1984).

General principles for designing a proportional syllabus

The phases of language program development are shown in Figure 9.1. The initial step is a needs survey, for reasons already discussed. Once it has been carried out, the purposes for a given second language program or course become much more clear. It is possible at this stage to draw up a written description of purpose, or, if a written document seems unnecessary, one may simply form a clear idea of what the purpose is and, if several teachers are involved, agree upon it. It is frequently useful to have the description of purpose written up, for later reference in program evaluation and/or modification, and as a reminder of assumptions made at an early stage.

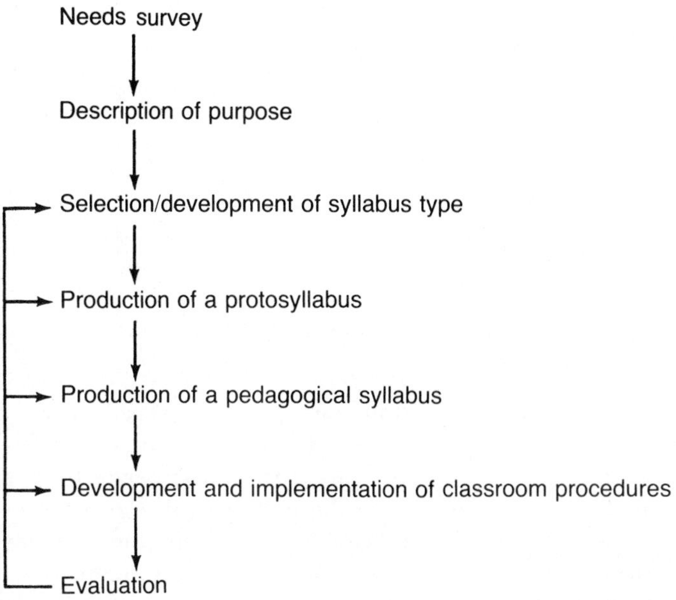

Needs survey

↓

Description of purpose

↓

→ Selection/development of syllabus type

↓

→ Production of a protosyllabus

↓

→ Production of a pedagogical syllabus

↓

→ Development and implementation of classroom procedures

↓

— Evaluation

Figure 9.1 Stages in language program development. (Based on Yalden 1983: 88.)

Choice of a syllabus type

After the description of purpose, and before the production of the pro-tosyllabus, I include a step that had been omitted by others working on syllabus design. The selection or development of a syllabus *type* now seems an essential part of the process. In Chapters 6, 7, and 8 I have discussed a range of types that have been proposed, organized according to different principles. The balanced or *proportional* type is the one from which the second-language-teaching frameworks described in Chapter 10 were produced. It has two advantages: It allows the course designer freedom to respond to changing or newly perceived needs in the learners; and at the same time it produces a *framework* for the teacher who wants to start out with a plan. A proportional syllabus type can give rise to many kinds of frameworks; and a framework can be designed for most second language teaching situations.

Once the syllabus type is determined, the content of the course can be prepared. Next, from the rather crude lists that usually make up the protosyllabus, a pedagogical syllabus is prepared. The contents of the protosyllabus are broken up (into groups of linguistic items, topics, functions, rhetorical skills – whatever has been included initially). These

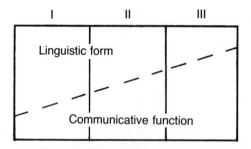

Figure 9.2 An example of the proportional approach to course design. (Based on Yalden 1983: 122.)

are arranged into combinations of various sorts (the process is illustrated in Chapter 10) to form the outline of a particular course. When this breakdown has been completed, and the particular course begins to take on form and substance, one can turn to the matter of classroom procedures for a specific classroom. The last phase is evaluation – of the course, of the learning achieved, and so on. At all stages in the process, feedback to previous steps takes place.

The procedure is dynamic, not static. Without feedback, one would end up with extremely rigid course outlines, and this is exactly what one is trying to avoid in contemporary course design. This is a most important point, which is not always accorded the importance it deserves. It is often difficult in the busy and demanding job of language teaching to take the time to reflect on what one is doing and to communicate one's ideas to one's colleagues. But to ensure that the purpose of the instruction is constantly borne in mind, and to mold the classroom work to it, is an essential goal.

Maintaining the balance

A brief illustration of how the proportional approach to overall course design works might be useful. Let us take the case of a general ESL course, beginning at an elementary level of communicative competence. One might begin with grammar and pronunciation only, as one does in a structural approach, but introduce work in the language functions and in discourse skills fairly early, and in time increase this component of the course. (See Figure 9.2.) For the purpose of keeping the diagram simple at this stage, only two components of language are represented: form and communicative function. One can, of course, produce much more complicated figures, showing the proportion of time and emphasis devoted to any number of components. I will assume that the term "function" here includes the communicative and rhetorical functions of language. Thus the sociolinguistic component is omitted – but only for the reason given: simplicity. The study of grammar would nonetheless remain in sharper focus through the first level of the program or course than would the study of functions and discourse skills.

At the next level, teaching interpersonal and textual areas gains increasing prominence, but teaching grammar also continues to occupy an important place. At the third level of this hypothetical course sequence, the balance shifts again. At this point in the sequence, work on communicative and discourse functions of language predominates, and one would expect linguistic form to be considered only as the need arises.

The place of ideational meaning

In this representation of the relationship between the emphases given to kinds of meaning in a syllabus, the whole area of notions and topics (the ideational layer of meaning) is not shown as a separate component. The choice of a given number of topics is inevitable in today's teaching, as very few individuals would advocate a return to teaching grammar and vocabulary items without a situation or context in which they might be used – however these might be determined. Topics, situations, general notions, themes can therefore be seen as the frameworks that provide support for the rest of the components that are included. Topics and situations will arise from a needs survey; this component is thus the least troublesome to fit into the design of a course.

Establishing the proportions

In using a balanced or proportional syllabus, there is no strict separation between teaching formal and functional areas. The divisions shown in Figure 9.1 represent differences in the proportion of time and emphasis devoted to a given component. They do not indicate that the two must always be kept separate. Indeed, it is assumed that it is usually impossible to do so.

The fully developed proportional model (Figure 9.3) includes the provision of an initial phase, principally comprising formal meaning. This phase is for complete beginners and need not last long; it provides them with some basic knowledge of the systematic or categorical side of language, before they go on to a more interactive mode of learning. Absolute beginners cannot be expected to solve communication problems (Allwright 1979: 170), and so this is almost essential as a starting point.

A study carried out by Bialystok lends further support to the argument for a more-or-less prolonged initial phase devoted to linguistic competence. She found that linguistic competence ("formal mastery") strongly interacts with strategic competence. To use strategies appropriately, there has to be a minimal level of proficiency in the second language (Bialystok 1983: 115). The length of this phase, and when and how it

Frameworks for second language course design

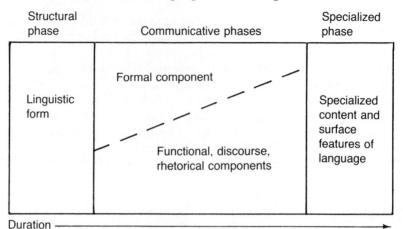

| Structural phase | Communicative phases | Specialized phase |

Structural phase — Linguistic form

Communicative phases — Formal component / Functional, discourse, rhetorical components

Specialized phase — Specialized content and surface features of language

Duration ⟶

Figure 9.3 Fully developed proportional model. (Based on Yalden 1983: 124.)

will blend in with a subsequent proportional phase, depends upon the circumstances in which the second language program is being conducted. Learners' own observations should whenever possible be taken into account; and when they are, the process of course design becomes interactive (cf. Candlin 1984).

Allowance can thus be made for the difficulty of broaching communicative and discourse functions explicitly with learners who have no knowledge at all of the target language. It also accommodates the position that although communicative competence includes linguistic competence, it is possible to teach grammatical competence *before* teaching sociolinguistic and discourse competence (cf. Canale 1983). The proportional model permits a change, nevertheless, to emphasis on speech acts and discourse skills in oral language at a relatively early stage. Once communicative work in oral language has been attended to sufficiently, it is possible to shift the emphasis once more: At more advanced levels, the syllabus designer can turn to rhetorical functions, especially in written language, as well as to recurrently troublesome surface features of language. A return to some work on form (to the "synthetic" approach, to use Wilkins's term) is also possible, once communicative performance is under way. Finally, the model can be extended to include more purely instrumental or "experiential" learning in subject areas (see Allen 1980 for discussion of experiential learning).

The proportional syllabus

The proportional syllabus is a model that can be used where neither immersion nor the sheltered classroom format is possible, but where development of overall competence is desirable. It is an attempt to include a number of components, to be treated systematically and nonsystematically. It is a rejection of the globally systematic as well as the globally nonsystematic approach (see Johnson 1980, 1982, for a full discussion of this distinction). The organization tends to be semantic rather than formal. The linguistic component is treated systematically in early stages and nonsystematically in later ones. The component that provides continuity is the theme, which constitutes a framework for several units or modules of instruction.

The theme is chosen according to the needs and wishes of the learners, and several themes may be used during a single language course. They may be subject-matter related in an educational context, but may equally well be job-related or of general interest. Topics and activities provide the focus and content of individual units or modules. This pattern of organization implies a task-oriented methodology, but because a general theme is present, the tasks are often enveloped in a simulation related to the theme. Within each module proportions can be varied to ensure balance between linguistic accuracy and communicative fluency (Brumfit 1980, 1984b) – that is, between control of structure and of communicative appropriateness.

General principles for designing frameworks

A framework as defined above is thus used in course design to cope with the several strands of communicative proficiency to be developed in the learner. Because there is so much current research relevant to course design, changes from time to time are inevitable and should be welcomed. But it is desirable to be able to assess the implications carefully before changing an entire design. Using frameworks permits this kind of flexibility. Furthermore, the use of frameworks recognizes that teachers have a major influence over what happens in the classroom (cf. Brumfit 1984b: 314). Thus a framework is not a completed structure for classroom interaction, but rather allows for a substantial contribution from teachers as it is developed for use in a particular instance.

Four general principles should be followed in preparing a framework. Briefly stated, these are that

1. both the design of the framework and its final product, the language course, should be conducted with as much consultation as possible with all those involved
2. the framework must necessarily be kept lean, and any tendency to do teachers' work for them should be resisted
3. the framework must be written so that it may be adapted easily
4. the framework should take into account available resources.

These four principles are elaborated below. Chapter 10 will present concrete examples of their application to a number of instructional contexts.

Interactive course construction

In Chapters 6 and 7, in discussing the rapport between linguist and teacher and in looking at the teacher's role in course design, I presented five sorts of relationship that might obtain. For the purposes of designing frameworks, the *interactive* relationship is the most productive (see Figure 6.2). Not only the employer or parent or client, but also the learner (who may in fact be the client) should be consulted and involved in the design process. This idea is sometimes a surprising one, both to children who are not used to being consulted about the content of language courses, and to adults, who expect the language teacher to have all the knowledge required to plan and execute a course. Yet if one is to take language use as the guiding principle, it follows that users must be consulted. It often requires some delicacy, and this matter will be given more detailed treatment in Chapter 11, in the section on needs analysis. Generally speaking, once they have understood what is being requested and why, both children and adults can happily and easily make the kind of contribution one would hope for. I am referring not only to the usual information about their background and interests, but also about their learning styles and preferences, of vital importance in the preparation of a framework.

If a framework is being prepared for use by a large number of teachers to produce a variety of different courses (see, e.g., p. 111), it may be necessary to use a sample of information from potential or typical learners. Trying to gather comprehensive information on all possible learners who would ever be taught using the framework being designed might be quite unrealistic. Nevertheless, some idea of who the learners are and what kind of proficiency they are interested in acquiring is necessary.

The third component (along with learner and teacher) will be the resources available. It seems impossible to ignore the presence or absence of various teaching and learning aids; yet it sometimes happens that in course design resources are called for which are simply not available. Using frameworks will avoid this problem, since they are not full-blown courses, but need to be interpreted variously according to the context. Interaction among all three elements in the design is necessary and must be ensured.

Leanness of initial design

One of the most difficult principles to adhere to, at first, is the principle of leanness in producing the units in a framework. The units are generally non–language-specific (that is, they can be used to produce courses for *any* second language). They are prototypes, not the finished product. They should *not* look like classroom-ready material. Getting material ready for a specific group of learners is a step that follows the preparation of the prototypical units. It is illustrated in Chapters 10 and 11.

Adaptability

A framework must be as flexible as possible. It must accommodate variation in teachers' styles as well as in learners' preferences. It will consist of a number of units, created on the basis of data yielded by the analysis of language needs. These units may be based on discourse categories, on topics or situations, or on tasks. For each, a number of communication objectives will be described. And for each objective, in turn, a large number of teaching and learning strategies and techniques will be specified, from which the teacher and the learner will choose as *together* they develop a course. The number of courses that might be produced from a given framework is limited only by the number of teaching/learning situations based on it. Furthermore, the same framework may be used to design courses for learners at various stages, by grading tasks and activities. In other words, a framework can be used in several contexts.

Resources

Finally, it is a principle of designing frameworks that one should make use of resources that are already available. Thus, for example, situation-based frameworks are designed to be used with general reference materials and books on teaching techniques and learning strategies, language-specific grammars, textbooks and dictionaries, as well as laboratory facilities. These resources are all available for that particular context.

However, for the discourse-based framework, only one language is involved. The list of resources is much smaller. It is equally indispensable, nonetheless. Part of the job is identifying how much is already at hand, and what is left to be done. In some situations, very little is available. In others, there is a wealth of material at hand. In preparing frameworks, resource availability must be studied and the knowledge of what there is built in to the design.

Following these principles, a great variety of frameworks can be designed. In Chapter 10, three that have been produced and from which several courses have been designed and taught will be described. In Chapter 11, to round off this introduction to second language course

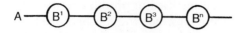

Figure 9.4 A string of theme-linked modules. A = thematic and topical elements (the "string"); B = linguistic and interactional elements (the "beads"). (Based on Yalden 1984: 19.)

design, techniques of needs analysis, matters of general methodology, and particular teaching techniques will be discussed.

Linking up the modules

The application of these principles of syllabus design produces theme-linked modules. A sort of beading occurs, where the theme is the string, and the modules represent beads of topics and tasks that elicit certain behavior (Figure 9.4). Within each bead, a proportional approach is maintained, and the whole string can be arranged so as to represent a proportional shift from form to function (in general education, for example), or from function to form (in adult education or ESP courses). Organization of the thematic and topical elements follows a chronological or logical linear progression. The linguistic and interactional elements are organized proportionally and spirally, and as a function of feedback from the learners. Form may predominate initially and the emphasis shift to communicative, discourse, or rhetorical functions later. The shifts can occur often, and are not confined to any particular level of instruction, nor are they always predictable. The teacher may attempt to place them in sequence and control them, for the sake of having a plan with which to enter the classroom, but should be prepared to modify the plan where and when necessary.

This form of organization produces a framework within which the teacher can work, making plans for classroom interaction as he goes along. It will exert a steering effect, and will be more effective if all users of the framework have had some participation in its preparation. It most certainly is not a method, but an approach to bridging the gap between the first phase of syllabus design (specification of content) and the second (classroom methodology and materials).

In spite of this description of frameworks from the teacher's perspective, it has to be remembered that *using* a language is not stringing together separate bits of linguistic form in order to arrive at a pleasing design. The whole purpose of using an interactive methodology is to avoid having the learner treat language as an assemblage of isolated units. Thus, while teachers in planning a course may very well select modules and arrange them in a sequence, learners will do no such thing when they are engaged in communication. For them, and for the teacher, the structure of classroom interaction can better be compared to the structure of a molecule, a group of atoms that are always in movement, always affecting one another. Though separate modules can be prepared to treat various aspects of language, they have to interact with each other for language to be produced and exchanges of meaning to take place. Only in preparation for teaching can the constituent parts be separated; they must necessarily come together once linguistic interaction begins.

Transposing

A final word about frameworks: It should be emphasized that although they may be written in English (as are those that appear in this work), they need not be intended, culturally or linguistically, to refer only to English-language environments. This is not to say that frameworks for a single target language could not be written − in fact, one of the three sets of frameworks so far produced was written for Bahasa Indonesia only. The other two, however, were prepared for use by teachers of several target languages. Examination of the case studies and samples from the frameworks will make this clear (see Chapters 10 and 11 and Appendixes A and B).

10 Three case studies

I have argued so far that today's second language teachers can have a good deal of choice when planning a course. This includes choice of

- an appropriate role
- the degree to which they work with linguists
- a model for syllabus and course design
- teaching techniques

I have attempted to make clear what some of the options now are. I have also described a particular syllabus type, involving particular choices.

In what follows, I will present three case studies that will illustrate how the proportional syllabus type can be used to produce frameworks, which in turn are to be used by many teachers to produce their own courses.

The three case studies represent three problems to be solved. In each instance a different solution was found. Each of the contexts will be examined with a view to tracing how decisions were made regarding the type of framework to be produced, and what exactly was produced in the end. Each framework will be illustrated by samples of units or prototypical units that were designed.

The first case study is of a framework designed for a particular language – Bahasa Indonesia. The other two studies are of frameworks that are not specific to any language, that is, they are used to prepare courses in *either* a number of languages that were specified before the framework was designed (see section titled "Task-Based Frameworks") *or* any number of languages at all (see section titled "Situation-Based Frameworks"). The examples of prototypical or actual units are written mostly in English. The inclusion of language other than English in the materials reproduced in this work is intended to illustrate the flexibility of the concept of the framework – understanding of the languages in question is not necessary for understanding of how the frameworks function. As I pointed out earlier, the most important aspect of the frameworks is that they *precede* the preparation of any specific language course for any specific group of learners. Once they are established, they can be "transposed" into any language, a process described in detail in the section "Situation-Based Frameworks." If the target language is English, the transposition will be that much more direct – but not much, since very little purely *linguistic* material is included in the frameworks.

Each of the three frameworks presented has a somewhat different focus. In the first, discourse competence is highlighted. In the second, the situation is the basis of the design, but the focus may shift from strategic to discourse to sociolinguistic competence, as the teacher and the learner desire. In the third, the emphasis is squarely on tasks that have to be carried out. The following outline may help to clarify these differences.

Case Study 1: Bahasa Indonesia for foreign service personnel and their spouses
Syllabus type: proportional and interactive
Main learning objective: ability to control discourse
Language to be taught: Bahasa Indonesia

Case Study 2: General and/or job-specific courses for adults
Syllabus type: proportional and interactive
Main learning objective: ability to function in a variety of situations
Languages to be taught: any

Case Study 3: Work-related courses for foreign service officers
Syllabus type: proportional and interactive
Main learning objective: performance of tasks through use of the target languages
Languages to be taught: Spanish, Arabic, Russian, Japanese, Chinese

Discourse-based frameworks

The context

The initiative for the preparation of the discourse-based framework came from the Department of External Affairs of the Government of Canada. The designers of the framework were two linguists, aided by a research assistant and a native speaker of Bahasa Indonesia.[1] The learners were to be Djakarta-based personnel and their spouses who had little or no knowledge of the target language, and who required functional proficiency in it as quickly as possible. Although grammars of Bahasa Indonesia were available to the teachers, they needed an approach to developing overall communicative competence in their learners.

The needs survey consisted of several interviews with the Language

1 See Yalden (1983, 1984) for further description of the project, and Yalden and Jones (1984) for the full text of this framework.

Training Branch of the Department of External Affairs, followed by interviews with seven recently returned employees of that department and their spouses. During these interviews, the linguists and their research assistant determined that the most urgent needs were for language to be used in a fairly predictable sequence of events that occur in the lives of foreign service personnel upon arrival in Djakarta: arriving at the airport, getting to a hotel, getting settled in their accommodation, going about the city, meeting people. The needs were not job-specific, but rather for general daily life during the posting. Material sufficient for at least sixty hours of instruction was required.

The objective was largely to provide learners with linguistic tools to manage life in the early stages of a posting abroad, and also provide the option of refining their knowledge and skill at a later stage. The possibility of "revisiting" the materials from time to time had to be built in. The teacher would need to be able to round out and supplement the information provided in the units, progressively making the language more difficult.

Teaching constraints

Learners were to be taught on a one-to-one basis or in very small groups. Teaching might or might not be intensive. Much depended on the time available to the learners before they left on posting. The teacher was to be a native speaker of the target language, who would not necessarily be a trained second language teacher.

The courses were to be given in classrooms furnished by the Language Training Branch. These were well-equipped rooms, with audiovisual equipment available. Photocopying facilities were accessible without difficulty. The seating was flexible, the rooms a suitable size for small-group work, well lit, and so on. In other words, they were optimal physical conditions.

The frameworks: basic decisions

Given that a native speaker of the target language was going to be working on a one-to-one basis or with only two or three learners at a time, and given that structural grammars and also dictionaries of Bahasa Indonesia were available, it was decided that there would be little or no treatment of structure as such in this framework.

Some forms of Bahasa Indonesia would be supplied, chiefly as exponents of language functions, the assumption being that the teacher would provide as much additional material as was required or possible, given time constraints. Such forms as are given in these frameworks are there chiefly as signposts toward a fuller rendering of the functions included.

A vital part of the design is that there is to be no "hidden" material. Negotiation between teacher and learner on content and on activities was to be carried on from a basis of shared knowledge of what was possible and available. This decision meant that the booklet that was produced is addressed equally to the teacher and to the learner. There is no teacher's book, no learner's workbook, only a single volume, from which the two partners in this situation would produce their own course.

The package

The whole package of materials made available for the courses in Bahasa Indonesia contains four components:

1. The frameworks, in the form of a pedagogical handbook entitled *Communications Needs Course #1: Bahasa Indonesia* (Yalden and Jones 1984)
2. A tape recording prepared to accompany a unit on pronunciation
3. A short, basic grammar of Bahasa Indonesia
4. A large package of communicative activities keyed to the topical units of the Communications Needs Course (CNC). (There are several kinds of units, which will be described below.)

The grammar provided was a structural one; it was also the most compact and readily available. Given the short time available for the production of these frameworks, there was no question of writing a grammar, or even of spending very much time selecting one for pedagogical purposes (although many grammars of many different types were examined, to check information on the forms of the language). Teachers and learners could, if they wished, use a different text from the one supplied.

The structure of the frameworks

The framework is divided into three parts, all addressed to *both* learner and teacher. Here is the table of contents:

How to use the CNC; an introduction for learners and their teachers.

Unit 1
  The Sounds of Indonesian
  Basic Notions
  Managing a Conversation
Unit 2
  At the Airport
Unit 3
  Restaurants and Taxis
Unit 4

Staffing and Running a Household
Unit 5
  Meals at Home
Unit 6
  Shopping
Unit 7
  Finding Your Way Around
Unit 8
  Entertainment and Social Conversation

The introduction includes advice on how to use the CNC, plus a section explaining types of communicative activity appropriate to a course of this nature. It also explains that materials in Unit 1 may often be combined with the topical units (2–8) in performing the interactive tasks that make up the bulk of the suggested activities. Topical units may themselves be combined, in accordance with the idea of "molecular" use of frameworks by learners. Here is an extract from the CNC showing how this is displayed. It is the list of topics and of language functions, with the units in which they occur.

Topics	Unit
Personal identification	2
Travel	2
Meals	3, 5
Taxis, automobiles	3, 7
Traffic	3, 7
Hiring staff	4
Finding a house	4
Running a house	4, 5
Foods, beverages	5
Shopping, buying	6
Clothing, jewelry	6
Entertainment	8

Language functions	Unit
Asking for information	2, 3, 4, 6, 7, 8
Giving information	2, 3, 4, 7
Asking for assistance	2, 7
Ordering food, beverages	3
Disagreeing	3, 6
Promising	4
Giving instruction	2, 4, 5, 6, 7
Describing	4, 6
Polite conversation	1, 8

Stress is also laid on the responsibility the learners themselves have for a speedy arrival at the level of proficiency they desire, and for use of the elements in the "package." It is explained also that the language items in Units 2–8 are there as a springboard. The teachers using the CNC will provide many variations on the items supplied. The exponents are not only phrases to be memorized, but are intended to suggest a direction for development of vocabulary and grammar. Finally, it is pointed out that the CNC can be used not only as the basis for the basic sixty hours of instruction, but for many more besides.

Unit 1 is divided into three sections. The first is a conventional introduction to the sounds of the new language, with an accompanying tape recording. This was supplied only because no other similar material was available at the time for Bahasa Indonesia. In another instance, treatments of the sound system might be available, or teachers might wish to provide their own. The second part, "Basic Notions," is intended to provide learners with a small amount of the target language, which they use to convey certain notions or concepts that come up over and over again in conversation. This is how it is introduced in the CNC:

No matter where you are, or what you are talking about you need to be able to understand and express the notion of number or quantity, whether it is to say you have lost two suitcases, or to ask how many mangoes the cook has bought, or to write down a telephone number. So it is with the general notion of location, of where things and people are, and several other broad categories as well. You should memorize most of this language, and then work it into the exercises you will be doing with your teacher. (Yalden and Jones 1984: 1.9)

The notions treated in the CNC are numbers and quantity; properties and qualities (existence/nonexistence, presence/absence, possibility/impossibility, location, motion); time; colors; reference. These were chosen on the basis of the communicative needs of the learners, as determined through the interviews. For each notion, a small amount of basic language is provided. Here is the example for the notion of reference:

Reference

thing	barang
something	barang sesuatu
that thing	barang itu
this thing	barang ini
things	barang-barang

"Thing" can, of course, also be used in managing an interaction. It is included since native speakers of a language will usually use some such word to fill in a slot for a word they do not know. The vocabulary of the CNC was selected with communicative goals in mind, rather than with any idea of specialist areas to be treated.

107

Frameworks for second language course design

The third section of Unit 1, "Managing a Conversation," is intended to help learners manage the task of listening to and understanding Indonesian. Here, work in discourse analysis was drawn on for inspiration, especially studies which reveal that learners are not neutral in interactions, but require a greater ability to control them than they generally have been given credit for (Long 1983b). This section helps learners to

– get a speaker to slow down, repeat, clarify
– ask for assistance
– get the names of things
– indicate whether or not they understand

and so on. Once more the learners are directed to practice this language in the context of any one of the topical units, since it is intended to help them control the flow of language coming from the teacher. In other words, it puts the learner in the driver's seat – something of a role reversal.

For the seven contextual units, organization by topics seemed suitable since the situations in which the language would be used had been easily identified. In other types of frameworks, some other kind of organization might be preferable, as was the case in the other two described in this work. The topics and communicative functions are listed in the introduction for the learner, as shown earlier. Language structures are not listed, as it is assumed that most of them will arise out of the topics. Some vocabulary items, phrases, and notes on structure are provided in each unit, but these represent only a very basic amount of language. The learners are expected to elicit more from their teacher, as needed. A dictionary and a basic grammar are thus necessary components of any course of study based on the CNC Bahasa Indonesia. The following selections from Unit 3 will illustrate the organization of the topical units.

Unit 3   Restaurants and taxis

Communicative needs
You will want to be able to handle these topics:
1. Meals and refreshments at a restaurant
   Asking for a waiter; requesting a menu; ordering food and beverages; asking for your bill.
2. Taxis
   Giving and understanding directions; asking about a trip; negotiating the fare; asking for alternative means of transportation.

1. Meals and Refreshments at a Restaurant
   A. Managing a Transaction
   Where is the waiter?   Mana pelayannya?
   What do you want?   Mau makan apa?
                             Mau mintta apa?

108

	[mau = will]
I want the menu.	Minta daftar makanan.
I do not want...	Tidak mau makan. ...
but I will eat...	tapi mau makan. ...
I'm hungry.	Lapar.
I'm full.	Kenyang.
I am overfull.	Kekanyangan.
May I have the bill?	Boleh minta bonnya?
How much is it?	Berapa jumlahnya?

The vocabulary sections were developed with the help of a native speaker of Bahasa Indonesia. They are intended to provide some ideas for the teachers, and something for the learners to get started on. They can be expanded as much as time allows for. They can also be used for reading and pronunciation practice. They are simple word lists, a page or two in length.

The section on taxis is arranged in a similar fashion, beginning with Managing a Transaction (I want to go to ..., How much?, How much will it cost?, That's too much., I will pay 150 rupiah., Is this the way to ... ?, etc.), followed by traffic vocabulary (north, south, left, right, no left turn, too fast, too slow, car, bus, etc.). There is also a small functional section on directions from the main square to the Canadian Embassy (e.g., from here to ..., then straight until ...), again included as a sign-post to teachers and learners of the kinds of activities that can be devised.

The unit ends with a section on learning activities and tasks.

Learning activities and tasks
A. Preparation
Review numbers, currency, spelling.
Learn the days of the week.
B. Communication
Role plays
– Telephone for a reservation. Give your name (spell it), the time of arrival, the number in your party. Ask for confirmation.
– Enter the restaurant. Ask for table near the window. Ask for a menu.
– Order your meal, after asking what is available. Check the prices. Ask for your bill.
– You wish to go to the Embassy. Ask a taxi driver how long it will take. Make sure you agree on the price before you set off.
– Ask for directions from the Embassy to Glodak Plaza.
Interactive exercises
– Using the street maps that accompany Unit 3, ask your teacher how to get from the restaurant to the Embassy. Each of you will have the same map, but don't look at each other's copy. Each of you should trace the route being described in pencil. Ask for clarification as you need it. When you get to the Embassy, compare your map with your teacher's. Is the route the correct one?

Accompanying this particular unit is a map of Djakarta, some extracts from the telephone directory showing restaurants, and some further map-reading and direction-asking and -giving exercises. For each contextual unit, there are a number of appropriate interactive exercises and tasks and activities. The aim of all of these is consistent with the overall goal of developing the learner's ability to get what he wants, in a variety of situations. Teachers may supplement what is supplied *ad infinitum*, as long as they stick to the general principles. When this framework was being prepared, two research assistants who knew the project well provided considerable assistance in compiling teaching/learning activities.

Summary

The discourse-based framework for Bahasa Indonesia courses is a set of materials from which the learner and the teacher together will derive the lessons by a process of negotiation. The learner's expectations and preferences are to be taken into account as the lessons evolve; these may include some study of the structures of the target language together with drills of various kinds. The CNC itself is very flexible and not meant to be studied unit by unit. One could start with any of the seven topical units, although they happen to be arranged in a chronological sequence of utility, gauged from point of arrival in the foreign country.

Once learners have gone through the introductory unit with the teacher and have become acquainted with the language for basic notions and for managing a conversation, they may direct their own learning to a very large extent. Working with the teacher, they select the units they want to study and the order in which they want to study them. They will supplement the CNC as needed with work from the grammar and with use of a dictionary.

Learners also have considerable input, if they wish, into the selection of learning and teaching techniques, and indeed should be encouraged to express their preferences, their satisfaction or lack of it, their feelings of confidence in certain areas or need for more practice in others. This is what is meant by deriving the lessons by a process of negotiation: Learners create their own lessons using the resources provided by teacher and linguists. The CNC is not a textbook, but the raw material on which teacher and learner work together to bring a course to life.

Follow-up

These discourse-based frameworks have been used as planned. No formal evaluation was carried out, but the degree of satisfaction with the course design was high on the part of the client, the learners, and the teachers, and led to further development of the general approach. Two subsequent projects, resulting in two different kinds of frameworks, are described in the next two sections.

Situation-based frameworks

The context

The situation-based frameworks had their genesis in the need for courses in a large number of different languages (including English) for a wide range of learners. The courses were to be offered by the Centre for Applied Language Studies at Carleton University,[2] whose clients might be government departments or agencies, industry, or private individuals. The courses had to be prepared quickly, with relatively little advance knowledge of what languages would be required at what times. There was often very limited lead time to prepare courses, and little or no information on the learners before they showed up in the classroom. Learners all had communicative needs, however, which meant that purely structural courses would not be adequate and would be rejected by the clientele for the courses. Needs of similar learners had been examined over the years, through questionnaires administered sporadically, through information collected from learners during the course of other classes, and through contact with the clients or sponsors. University administrators who were familiar with the kinds of learners to be served were also interviewed. A picture of need emerged for language for travel on tours or on business, for coping with general daily needs in a foreign country, and for job-specific purposes. The variety was great, as was the requirement to provide courses to match the learners' needs and wants. The possibility of a needs analysis or survey that would specify course objectives in any remotely definitive way was evidently excluded.

Teaching constraints

The courses were to be offered in the evening, in the context of a program in continuing education, or during the days or evenings either at the university or on the clients' premises. Because these second language courses were not part of the university's regular offerings, teachers could not count on the usual language classrooms being available. This meant that courses could not be designed for use in fully equipped audiovisual classrooms with videotape recorders and the like. The most that could

2 The Centre for Applied Language Studies at Carleton University serves the modern language departments and the Department of Linguistics, and runs all ESL courses. It provides courses on contract as well, for which the situation-based frameworks were developed.

be expected was use of the photocopying machines, and since many of the teachers worked elsewhere and arrived at the university or at the clients' offices shortly before the class, time for photocopying was limited. Tape recorders were easily available, and both teachers and learners were accustomed to using them.

Teachers were to be native speakers of the target languages. Although they had all had experience teaching, they were not likely, under the circumstances, to have the necessary materials already prepared. Furthermore, in some cases, they had had little or no training in communicative approaches to second language instruction or in the preparation of courses for specific purposes.

For many of the languages to be taught, there were no materials available other than a structural grammar and a dictionary. There were occasional tape recordings, usually of audiolingual drills, and there was a possibility in many instances of collecting authentic materials in the target languages.

The frameworks: basic decisions

The description of purpose that had emerged from the preliminary and sketchy needs survey was of general as well as job-specific courses for adults. There were to be two levels, and as many as twenty-five languages might be involved (in fact, at the time of writing, thirty have been taught using these situation-based frameworks). To determine the approach to be taken, a working group was established. In order to provide a co-operative analysis of the context and a fruitful response to it, the participation of linguists, teachers of several languages, experienced materials writers, and administrators was needed.[3] The main working group of six individuals frequently invited colleagues to join in the discussion, and by the time the materials writers began to produce the definitive prototypical units, a great many people had been consulted. This is typical of the project. Feedback was continually sought and received, and indeed this is still the case.

The point of departure for this group was the proportional model for syllabus design and the *Communication Needs Course in Bahasa Indonesia*. Our original position was to have teachers as members of the working group who would, working with the linguists and materials writers, produce a series of language-specific courses, along the lines of the *CNC Bahasa Indonesia*. This turned out to be impossible for several reasons:

---

3 The nucleus of the working group were Joyce Pagurek, Brigid Fitzgerald, Alister Cumming, George Chouchani, and myself. Devon Woods also joined us from time to time.

1. We did not know which languages would be required first by learners sent to us by external clients.
2. We could therefore not select the teachers who should be members of the working group.
3. We had neither time nor resources to produce an indefinite number of courses.

We therefore asked the materials writers to take on the job of trying to work up some non–language-specific units that would resemble the units for Bahasa Indonesia, *but that would have no target language forms in them.* These units would be written in English, of course, but would be intended to serve as prototypes for any number of second language courses for the purposes of our learners. We decided to ask several teachers to join the group, and selected speakers of Arabic, Mandarin, Portuguese, and Swahili, who also happened to be trained teachers of ESL. We were later joined by a teacher of French who was familiar with our approach. The materials writers, responding to the challenge, finally arrived at a sort of distillation of their experience (which had been entirely in producing materials for ESL), and moved another step away from the idea of a classroom-ready module or unit – in fact, to the stage of the protosyllabus, or prototypical unit.[4]

These units seemed satisfactory to the participating teachers, who then took them away, and began the task of preparing *transpositions* (not translations) into the target languages for which they were responsible, and also *for the groups for which they were responsible.* There was thus a dual level of transposition: one linguistically and culturally neutral, the other sociolinguistically marked according to the needs of the learners involved.

The frameworks that have resulted are not intended to be language-specific. The working group concentrated on content for our courses primarily at a semantic level, without examining linguistic forms for particular languages. We began with the ideas and concepts to be included in the entire series of frameworks and then let the teachers worry, during the transposition phase, about what the linguistic forms would be, what the cultural background for their course should be like (French for English speakers going to Quebec? or to France? or both?), what is socially appropriate in China, Portugal, Tanzania, or Ontario. Only in

---

4 The first drafts of the units produced now look like realizations in English of the current set of prototypical units. The initial drafts are thus the outcome of a process already implicit in them. They were rejected by the teachers in the group because they were too much like classroom-ready materials, and the teachers found them confining. These teachers told the materials writers they were inhibited by the amount of cultural content in the *language forms* suggested in the draft units, and that they found themselves trying unsuccessfully to translate the English exponents provided.

this way could we accommodate all the sociolinguistic needs, known and unknown, that might arise.

In summary, a project was set up with the following objectives:

1. A framework for the application of sociolinguistic analyses of communication needs was to be developed. Using questionnaires and interviews with learners and employers, data would be gathered on the linguistic/communicative needs of prospective students of a number of different languages. These data would be analyzed to determine the situations, topics, functions that would be most useful to the learners.

2. A handbook addressed *only to teachers (unlike* the Bahasa Indonesia framework), treating the use of the frameworks. It was plain that these situation-based frameworks were more abstract, linguistically, than the CNC *Bahasa Indonesia,* and were specifically for teachers' use. (This is not to say that the learners could not have input into the course – see p. 118).

3. A basic introductory set of units would be produced to introduce a minimum of language covering basic notions, the ability to manage discourse, and some general coping strategies.

4. A long series of other units would be produced, on the basis of data yielded by the analysis of language needs. A large number would be needed, to ensure that teachers could choose what they wanted to produce a course geared to the needs of the moment.

5. Since topics and situations would be more easily identifiable than tasks, and since discourse skills would be introduced in the introductory units, topics and situations would be used as the focus for each unit.

6. For each unit, a series of communication objectives would be described. Learners and teachers would again *together choose* appropriate objectives for the specific course being taught.

7. A large number of teaching/learning strategies and techniques would be described for each unit. The learner and the teacher would, once more, choose from these resources as together they developed a second language course.

See Appendix B for concrete examples of actual situation-based frameworks.

In the interactive approach to the design of *specific courses,* these situation-based frameworks bear a resemblance to their precursor, the discourse-based frameworks. However, it cannot be said that these situation-based frameworks are addressed directly to the learner, as were the earlier ones. Thus these frameworks are closer than the first ones to being materials for teachers only; and indeed, as time went on, teacher-training elements were added to the total "package."

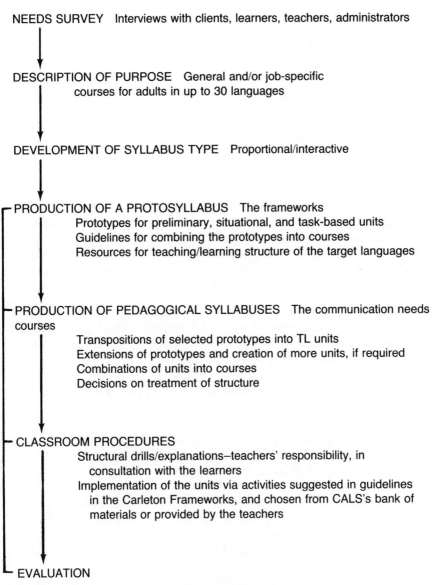

NEEDS SURVEY   Interviews with clients, learners, teachers, administrators

DESCRIPTION OF PURPOSE   General and/or job-specific
         courses for adults in up to 30 languages

DEVELOPMENT OF SYLLABUS TYPE   Proportional/interactive

PRODUCTION OF A PROTOSYLLABUS   The frameworks
         Prototypes for preliminary, situational, and task-based units
         Guidelines for combining the prototypes into courses
         Resources for teaching/learning structure of the target languages

PRODUCTION OF PEDAGOGICAL SYLLABUSES   The communication needs
courses
         Transpositions of selected prototypes into TL units
         Extensions of prototypes and creation of more units, if required
         Combinations of units into courses
         Decisions on treatment of structure

CLASSROOM PROCEDURES
         Structural drills/explanations–teachers' responsibility, in
            consultation with the learners
         Implementation of the units via activities suggested in guidelines
            in the Carleton Frameworks, and chosen from CALS's bank of
            materials or provided by the teachers

EVALUATION

Figure 10.1 The CALS (Carleton) frameworks.

The package

The provision of a number of components, not only the frameworks, was required in this case in order to get from the prototypical units to classroom interaction. Figure 10.1 illustrates the relationship between the *process* of course design and its *product* in terms of actual second-

115

language courses. It shows the steps of language program development applied specifically to the context under consideration here, and that resulted in the writing of the Carleton Frameworks (see Appendix B). It is clear that various tools are required at various levels of the work, and that these would be provided by a number of different individuals, both within the working group and outside it. The contributions become more and more concrete, more specific to the individual learner, as the process reaches its conclusion.

For the implementation of the situation-based frameworks, the components listed below were finally determined to be necessary. The list is long, and obviously it would have been difficult to assemble everything at once before beginning to work with the frameworks. The decision was therefore to concentrate on six or seven languages initially (other than ESL, for which a very good resource center existed already). In other situations, the "stocks" could be built up for one language at a time. (For ESL, if financial resources are no object, there is certainly no lack of materials. A large collection of language-specific materials could be assembled very rapidly.) Here is the list of what was required.

The frameworks
1. A guide for the users. This would include a booklet or booklets, addressed to the learners and to the teachers, describing the system and giving suggestions on how to use it.
2. A guide addressed specifically to teachers.
3. Three units called "Expressing Basic Concepts," "First Steps Toward Communication," and "Coping Strategies."
4. The situation-based prototypical units.
5. Notes on how to prepare an introduction to pronunciation.
6. Sample lessons in several languages (classroom-ready material, produced by the teachers in the working group, which can be added to later on).
7. Videotapes of communicative classes in ESL, demonstrating a range of teaching techniques. The range is to be specified in advance and various levels of proficiency filmed.
8. As large a collection as possible of culturally neutral teaching materials and aids, geared to the units.
9. As large a collection as possible of books containing ideas for communicative activities for second language teaching. These would be mostly for ESL, since more work has been done for English than for any other language. They would serve as references for teachers, and could include textbooks.

Language-specific teaching/learning materials
1. Reference grammars for teachers, and learners' grammars

TABLE 10.1 WORKSHEET FOR SITUATION-BASED FRAMEWORKS

Materials to be produced	*Phase I: basic*	*Phase II: TL counterparts*
Introductory modules		
1. Basic Concepts (booklet)	X	X
2. Basic social skills (i.e., First Steps Toward Communication) (booklet)	X	X
3. Managing discourse (i.e. Coping Strategies) (booklet)	X	X
4. Phonology (booklet and tapes)	O	X
5. How to use the modules (booklet and videotape)	X	O
6. Effective Learning Strategies (booklet and videotape)	X	O
Situational modules		
1. List of general themes for which units are to be written (e.g., travel)	X	O
2. List of topics appropriate to each theme for which units are to be written	X	O

2. Dictionaries
3. References on phonology
4. Realia, authentic material (print and nonprint).

Evaluation and feedback procedures
1. Non–language-specific (i.e., on the frameworks themselves)
2. Language-specific (i.e., regarding actual courses)

Once the working group had defined the total package, the next steps were to (a) continue production of the prototypical units and (b) begin to assemble the other resources. The latter process is a long one; I shall return to it shortly.

The structure of the frameworks

The relationship of the frameworks to the language-specific courses requires some further refinement. Table 10.1 is a worksheet that was used to aid in the decisions on responsibilities to be spread among the members of the group. It divides the work into two phases: basic (e.g., the production of the frameworks) and target language counterpart (i.e., production of actual language courses). The sheet makes it appear that all this took place in an orderly manner – it did not. The courses began

TABLE 10.2 OBJECTIVES, EXPONENTS, ACTIVITIES

	Phase I: basic	Phase II: TL counterparts
1. Communication objectives. About six objectives per unit, stated in paragraph form. These can be arranged as stages in a typical interaction.	X	O
2. Sample exponents. Provided in English for transposition into target languages.	X	X
3. Communicative activities appropriate to each module. The Phase I modules are to include a list of appropriate activities from which the teacher (and the learner) will choose. Sometimes the activities will need to be reworked or reinterpreted in the target language (e.g., role plays); but the initial choice is to be made from the Phase I modules. Phase II counterparts will appear much later and are not included at this point.	X	O
4. Criteria for choice of the activities are that they be chosen to develop the following abilities: – to express basic notions – to develop and use social skills – to manage discourse – to produce desired illocutionary effect – to use appropriate structures of the target language – to use appropriate lexis in the target language		

to shoot up around the production of the frameworks, since the teachers wanted to try each one as the materials writers finished it. Still, the plan was there, and it was followed more or less directly.

The format of each of the prototypical units had next to be decided. Using the CNC *Bahasa Indonesia* as a model, and consulting also *Threshold Level* (van Ek 1980) objectives, sample exponents and communicative activities were to be included, as shown in Table 10.2. Choice of the communicative activities clearly takes into account all the strands of second language proficiency present in the framework the research group was using (Canale and Swain 1980). In addition, as in the CNC *Bahasa Indonesia,* there is explicit reference to the development of ability

TABLE 10.3 LIST OF ITEMS REQUIRED FOR THE CALS FRAMEWORKS PROJECT
(TO 1985)

Written and published at Carleton University
1. Introductory booklet to the whole project
2. Teacher's Guide to using the Carleton Frameworks
3. Situation-based frameworks
4. Communication needs courses (CNCs) (these are language-specific and
   have been written for several languages, as the need arose)

Published materials available at CALS or belonging to teachers
1. for pronunciation
2. for grammar
3. for vocabulary
Authentic texts in target languages, as up-to-date as possible, gathered on an
ongoing basis by teachers, students, members of CALS.

---

to express basic notions. Exactly what kind of emphasis would be given
to each of these strands is not specified at this point. The proportions
would presumably vary from one course to another.

Extracts from these situation-based frameworks (see Appendix B)
show how the materials writers interpreted the decisions of the working
group. As units were produced, they were given to the teachers in the
group, who were asked to "transpose" them into their own language
and then to produce some classroom-ready materials based on them.
This part of the process is described in Chapter 11. Each teacher produced different materials, depending on the characteristics of the target
language and culture, and on the characteristics of the learners they
anticipated working with. *Every time a framework is used* one can expect
a different course to be produced. Teachers usually want to work things
out for themselves anyway. The frameworks help by (a) providing a
plan of attack in second language course design and (b) cutting down
preparation time by 20 to 50 percent.

Summary

Another worksheet, produced later in the project, will serve to summarize decisions regarding the CALS project up to the end of 1985.[5] It
shows the list of items required (Table 10.3).

---

5 As the project is still ongoing, further developments can be expected. The production
  of a communicative grammar to be tied in with the situation-based units is being
  contemplated. Elicitation of grammar from the language that is used in any given unit
  needs to be demonstrated in a booklet that would accompany the modules already
  available.

Follow-up

Work on the Carleton frameworks project has passed through several stages. It moved from an original position in which the teachers of the target languages working with the group were to produce a series of language-specific courses, to the current situation in which we have arrived at a distillation of the experience of the materials writers and the participating teachers, moving further back from the classroom-ready module. The working group has produced a set of directions to teacher and learner, who working together will be able to produce a very large range of classroom interactions. Thus, in the original descriptions of the project, the creation of a range of teaching materials is emphasized. Teacher training or preparation is mentioned briefly, but becomes more important, more central as the project goes on. At present, it is evident that these situation-based frameworks together with the supplementary materials in the Materials Bank represent a system for preparing teachers very rapidly to produce language courses with a highly communicative orientation.

The strands of second language proficiency (i.e., those identified in Chapter 2) are dealt with as follows:

Structural strand: Standard published materials and/or teachers' own
    materials, based on language actually used as the course progresses
Discoursal and strategic: three preliminary modules
Sociolinguistic: situational modules as realized for each target language
    and for each group of learners.

Responsibility for the proportional emphasis given to each strand must rest with the teacher using these frameworks. After an initial training session, working groups can be formed to allow teachers to exchange ideas, and informal contact will usually occur among teachers using these frameworks in any case. Teachers using the frameworks described here have been generous in assisting newcomers to tune in to the system, and this has greatly helped to initiate those who are not familiar with the approach. Reactions to the project are positive, as long as the teacher understands the principles on which it is based. It is quite evident that it would be an enormous mistake to put the prototypical modules into the hands of an unprepared teacher and expect him to do much with them. A period of preparation is essential, and this is being provided through workshops, and the preparation of further guides and video-tapes, which were foreseen as being a necessary part of the materials available.

The process of transposition, and the selection and use of the situational modules together with the preliminary modules to make up thematic courses, will be treated in Chapter 11.

Task-based frameworks

The context

The third project was begun, like the first, for the Department of External Affairs of the Government of Canada. It was to focus quite narrowly on the needs of Canadian government officials responsible for trade and commerce in embassies abroad. As before, an approach to syllabus design was needed that would take into account the characteristics of language as communication. This time, the work was to be carried out by two linguists (Maryse Bosquet and myself) working in consultation with the Language Programs Branch of the Department of External Affairs. The objective was to provide further frameworks in addition to the CNC *Bahasa Indonesia,* which was already finished and being used. The new frameworks were to enable teachers to give courses at the intermediate level in five languages: Spanish, Russian, Arabic, Chinese, and Japanese.

The needs analysis was much more extensive and yielded more specific data than in either of the two previous projects. Checklists were prepared, in order to gather authentic documents representative of the kinds of texts commercial officers have to be familiar with and to carry out interviews to identify aspects of the language the learners would want to master. The first objective was abandoned quite early. To gather documents representative of all the text types involved in the five languages would have taken much longer than the time available. The analysis of such a large amount of documentation would have constituted a major research task. Another reason also emerged: Such an analysis was not essential for our purposes. The adoption of a task-oriented syllabus type that would require considerable input from the learners simplified the approach considerably. I will return to this question later.

Quite a lot of information was already available, but most of it was of a general nature. Data were still needed that would permit development of

– a learner profile (who the learners were, to what extent a "common core" profile could be used, where discrepancies and/or similarities lay/diverged from a possible common core)
– an idea of what the language expectations of the posts abroad were, to attempt to determine the relationship between institutional needs and learners' needs and expectations
– an inventory of target tasks (see p. 124), that is, those tasks identified as required in order for an officer to function adequately in a particular target situation.

TABLE 10.4 TASK TYPES

---

1. Professional
   sell Canadian products
   promote importation of Canadian products
   assist in and carry on negotiations of contracts
   perform services for Canadian business
   deal on behalf of Canadian companies
2. Social/professional
   keep up conversation
   make pleasantries
   stimulate social conversation to put people at ease
3. Practical
   get around the city and country to which posted
   interact with people at airline desks, with taxi drivers, in banks
   order meals
   go shopping
   get laundry done
   etc.

Initially a set of checklists for each category was designed, to be used within a structured interview with a number of commercial officers. However, given the constraints of time and the large amount of information collected, the information was summarized from extensive notes taken during the interviews.

These were scheduled by the Personnel Operations Bureau, conducted in the commercial officers' offices, and lasted about an hour each. All the officers interviewed were career officers who had held one or more postings abroad in the target language situations covered by this project. A total of twelve individuals were interviewed. Once the interviews were over, the linguists spent several sessions analyzing their notes, using six categories (tasks, topics, settings, interlocutors, channel, skills or communication needs) to prepare a matrix showing the salient information for each category and the languages for which the information had been collected. The first four categories were further subdivided into categories labeled "professional," "social/professional," and "practical." The list of tasks is shown in Table 10.4. The needs from one language to another varied somewhat, with the most general use to be made of Spanish. However, since not all the officers interviewed agreed on the exact conditions for use of the target languages, and because of later decisions regarding the syllabus type, the information gathered at the time is not reproduced. The identification of tasks in itself turned out to be far more important.

The second category, topics, was quite vast. In general it had to do with international business, trade developments, export of manufactured goods, trade policy and relations, and so on. More specific topics could be anything from turbines and hydroelectric dams to interest rates, letters of credit, contracts to drill oil wells, the pulp and paper industry – a vast spectrum representing all of Canada's commercial and trade interests abroad. The physical settings included offices, hotels, trade fairs, agricultural tours, as well as restaurants and social gatherings. Another series of settings that were familiar to the two researchers included home, getting to work, the embassy, in the streets, shops.

The interlocutors would be primarily high-level government officials and businessmen. However, in many instances, farmers were included in the list – not surprising, given Canada's economy. Included in social settings were business contacts, official guests, friends; for practical purposes, domestic staff, salespersons, police, duty personnel, embassy drivers were included.

Analysis of channel of communication and text types turned out to be extremely useful. Here is the list:

Speaking	face-to-face
	by telephone
	through interpreters
	in discussion
Listening	face-to-face
	by telephone
	use of interpreters
	in discussion
	radio/television
Reading	newspapers, magazines
	reports
	official documents
	official correspondence
	public notices and signs
Writing	reports (i.e., checking translators' work)
	letters (i.e., checking translators' work)

From the interview data and from all of these matrices, further information on what were labeled (at this point in the project) "skills" was collected. Regarding how often these skills would be used, it emerged that writing was the least necessary. On the other hand, reading for information was a daily necessity. Reading to check for accuracy in translations of reports and correspondence prepared by secretaries and local staff, as well as reading letters and correspondence, was also considered useful by several of the officers interviewed. Listening was vital. It involved comprehension for various purposes, some predictable – such as using the telephone, listening to speeches, gathering specific information – but one of the principal purposes was the interesting one of monitoring the interpreter. Sometimes interpreters get off the track (deliberately or not) and have to be set back on it, and the understanding of nuance is important. Being able to follow quick exchanges between the interpreter and the person being interpreted is useful (and not illegitimate, since in many countries it is official policy to use interpreters for official meetings, whether the participants all speak the language of the host country or not). Finally, speaking was needed for two main purposes: making and responding to speeches at official receptions, and to carry on social conversation. Other purposes were expressed, but these were by far the predominant ones. Certain practical purposes (e.g., ordering meals) were also included.

Teaching constraints

The teaching constraints were virtually the same as for the discourse-based frameworks for Bahasa Indonesia. The same physical conditions and the same kinds of teachers were anticipated. Differences were that (a) for the five languages involved, there was already plenty of material available, particularly for Spanish; (b) the languages to be taught were known well in advance; (c) the groups of learners (again particularly for Spanish) might occasionally be larger than for the less-used languages; (d) lead time for preparation was greater; and (e) these task-based frameworks were to be for the intermediate level.

Basic decisions

Because the account of this project has to be arranged in a linear fashion for the reader, the steps seem discrete. In fact, they are not. All through the needs analysis, lively discussion of the syllabus type was going on, so that by the time it was complete, the decision to shape a task-oriented syllabus had been taken. A topic- or situation-based syllabus was out of the question. These categories were enormous, and the commercial officers could not see how we could ever specify situations or topics in great detail. They all wanted some room for structure – but it could not be the basis of the design, for reasons discussed already. Language functions were spread throughout the texture of the needs survey; there seemed no ready criterion for selecting them, since all functions needed to be taught, according to individual perception of need.

The kind of learner for whom these frameworks were being prepared was important in reaching the final determination to select tasks as the focus. One of the means of evaluation was to be quite simply whether or not the officers could perform tasks in the target language. This was

124

the chief criterion of success, and the one they were all most interested in. Thus, "task" seemed to be the best focus to use in

1. identifying learners' needs
2. defining syllabus content
3. organizing language acquisition opportunities
4. measuring student achievement.

"If 'task' will serve in all these capacities, it should provide the basis for naturally compatible decisions at all stages in program design and implementation" (Long 1985: 89).

"Task" in this project means nothing obscure. By "task" is meant "the hundred and one things people *do* in everyday life, at work, at play, and in between. 'Tasks' are the things people will tell you they do if you ask them and they are not applied linguists" (Long 1985: 89). As far as the future learners were concerned, tasks would mean something quite concrete and would be familiar objectives. Furthermore, the commercial officers would be able to provide an endless list of tasks and topics and settings to their teachers, who would then be able to organize learning acquisition opportunities and provide, so to speak, the necessary linguistic items *on the basis of information given to them directly by the learners.*

We had the inventory of tasks, and had produced a list of task types. From these, we would derive pedagogical tasks, and would suggest ways of selecting and sequencing the tasks to form a task-oriented course. (Long suggests that selection and sequencing the pedagogical tasks to form a task syllabus should be the final step, but since our objective was to provide a framework, and not the finished product, we decided only to suggest the organization, as in the project described in the section on situation-based frameworks.)

The framework produced as a result is the most flexible, the most interactive, and certainly the leanest of the three projects described. Of the three, it comes closest toward the minimalist approach adopted by Breen and Candlin. They state that "we need to acknowledge that any curriculum – including a communicative curriculum – cannot strictly be designed as a whole from the start . . . Any curriculum is a personal and social arena" (Breen and Candlin 1980: 106). "Language learning may be seen as a process which grows out of the interaction between learners, teachers, texts and activities" (Breen and Candlin 1980: 95). (See also Breen 1984; Candlin 1984.) The object was to provide a range of content that would activate process competences, but it could not be achieved without the help of the learners themselves. The principle of interactivity was to be applied as before – but extended to devolve major responsibility for topical content to the learner himself. The teacher would retain the role of provider of resources and creator of opportunities for second language learning.

The package

For this project, the package to be delivered to the client consisted of the prototypical units and a set of learning activities. Although a larger *total* package would be required in order to implement these task-based frameworks (something similar to the one for the situation-based frameworks), the responsibility of the linguists stopped at provision of the units and activities – at least for the duration of the initial project.

The prototypes were to have the following characteristics:

1. They were to be written in English.
2. They would constitute the raw material from which teacher and learner together would work.
3. They would consist of a set of tasks.
4. The description of each task would include a description of purpose.
5. A variety of teaching/learning techniques would be suggested.

As before, these task-based frameworks are not fully developed, language-specific courses. It would remain for the learner and the teacher to negotiate regarding the use of materials (within the limits of the time available), the learners' preferred strategies, and other resources available in the specific language being learned. Ultimately, one might envision the production of handbooks for each language being learned, along the lines of the *CNC Bahasa Indonesia*. However, initially, and indeed possibly forever, this would be unnecessary.

It was decided to abandon the preparation of modules for the "practical" aspects of language use, since the situation-based frameworks, already being written, would thoroughly cover this need. Accordingly, the linguists proceeded to the production of the prototypes.

Structure of the frameworks

Before the final prototypes were written, there were renewed discussions with the client. Representatives of the Language Training Branch had felt the prototypes should reflect actual language situations encountered by commercial officers abroad. However, our analysis had shown that the specification of actual language situations and tasks goes far beyond the mandate of the prototypical phase. The commercial officers confirmed, in further interviews, that the objectives specified for the prototypes reflected the skills they needed to develop and apply to a variety of situations and languages. They approved of the solution to the pedagogical problem and felt it was the only one possible. The emphasis on skills applied to tasks was appropriate, as the time allotted to learn the target language can be determined only by the learner's needs and the time the learner could in fact give to language training. Focus on skills would cover the major situations to be faced at the post. Focus on skills only seemed particularly desirable since, as one officer remarked, learners were not robots and could not be programmed to perform their tasks.

In the final document (Yalden and Bosquet 1984a), tasks are grouped together in categories labeled "skills." (The word "skills" was used in a particular sense, as an umbrella term to group task types together. The use of this word, a technical one in applied linguistics, did not perturb the client, and indeed was one that came out of the interviews with the officers.) The information displayed in the matrix of skills and tasks was further refined, and two categories were adopted:

1. Prototypes for the preparation of modules for developing skills in communication.
2. Prototypes for the preparation of modules to help learners *apply these skills to tasks* that would simulate on-the-job encounters in the target languages.

The list of prototypes comprises a core of units that respond to the most frequently cited communication needs as displayed in the matrix. Working from the matrix it would have been possible to design a very large number of pedagogical units, as many combinations suggested themselves. Only those that seemed most urgently required by the commercial officers were extracted. Table 10.5 shows the final list of the units. For each skill, frameworks were provided for the teacher and learner to use in planning lessons. Several of these are reproduced in Appendix A. They are extremely economical. They serve to define objectives for teaching/ learning interactions, and to focus the classroom work. Text types, drawn from the needs analysis, are suggested, and communication skills to be developed are listed succinctly. For each framework, a number of sample activities were attached.[6]

The production of what seems a highly skeletal presentation had taken a good many months' work. It is the result of a careful analysis of the communication needs of the clients, and of an examination of the possible pedagogical solutions. The language-specific courses that result would follow the proportional syllabus model, this time with major input from both learner, in terms of ideational content, and from teacher, in terms of methodology. In fact, the methodology would be the most important part of this project from the point of delivery of the frame-

6 Most of these were taken from textbooks listed in an appendix to frameworks, entitled "Useful References." See the "Summary and Follow-up" to this section for further comment on this aspect of the frameworks.

TABLE 10.5 THE FRAMEWORKS FOR DEVELOPING AND APPLYING
LANGUAGE SKILLS

A. Introduction: to the learner and the teacher
B. Using the frameworks
C. The frameworks for developing skills
   1. Monitoring oral and written texts
      a. Monitoring the development of an argument/discussion
      b. Monitoring to identify the communicative purpose/function of an interaction
      c. Monitoring an interpreter
      d. Monitoring for accuracy of content
   2. Reading for information
      a. Reading to get around
      b. Reading to keep abreast of current events
      c. Reading in order to react
   3. Using the telephone
      a. Communicative purposes
      b. Types of calls
      c. Examples of text types
   4. Opening and closing encounters in a variety of settings
   5. Handling information exchanges
   6. Participating in presentations on Canadian agriculture and industry
   7. Negotiating sales
D. Useful references

Source: Yalden and Bosquet (1984b).

works on – but the frameworks had to be produced before the methodology could be prepared and used.

Note, finally, that the units of the frameworks are not arranged in a hierarchy of either difficulty or potential usefulness. The learner should have input on the subject of usefulness; the teacher can make the classroom interactions more or less difficult according to the learner's needs. Thus the units can be recycled, as can indeed all the units in these frameworks, both for classes at different levels and to individualize the instruction – an important principle.

Summary and follow-up

Authentic materials from each target culture would be required. Assembling a supply of materials (newspapers, magazines, telephone directories, maps) would be helpful in transposing the prototypes to language-specific teaching situations. The more the prototypes can be made to fit into the target culture, the more effective the instruction should be.

Some preparation of learners not familiar with such an approach would be necessary. A briefing about the frameworks and a short handbook would be prepared for this purpose. Teachers would require preparation also, since they would not be familiar with the frameworks. They would either be experienced and therefore have their own views about how language should be taught, or inexperienced and therefore have little if any notion of how to proceed. A period of orientation for individuals using this approach was therefore essential.

A recommendation that the implementation of the frameworks should be very carefully monitored was submitted to the client. Also, suggestions regarding supplementary materials required were provided. The selection and use of these supporting elements of instruction should be supervised so as to develop a consistent approach and ensure that the learners have an adequate say in the process. Teachers, in other words, should not be allowed to assume a dominant role in the construction of the teaching program. Rather, the process is seen as three-way (see Figure 6.2, Chapter 6): linguist–learner–teacher (as part of the total resources available), working cooperatively. It was also stressed that attempts to "freeze" the kind of materials that should be produced would hamper their effectiveness, so that teachers should be encouraged to build up a bank of activity types and task types that could be drawn on by all those using these frameworks. At this point, the preparation of the frameworks was complete, and they were ready for delivery to the client.

11 Using frameworks

When a set of frameworks has been completed, the next phase is implementation – that is, their realization in the form of a real course for real learners. This involves a number of further steps. (1) A second needs survey is carried out. (The first, done before any frameworks are written, is usually a broader, more general survey than the teacher-conducted one.) (2) The modules that the teacher wants to use are selected and arranged. (3) General methodological decisions are taken, based on linguistic and psycholinguistic principles. (4) The prototypical units or modules have to be transposed into the target language, with appropriate consideration of cultural factors. (5) Last, classroom activities must be prepared.

Although the standard *stages* to be gone through are to be followed as outlined below, no standard *result* is to be expected. Each time a teacher or group of teachers uses a framework, a different course will result. In what follows, examples drawn from one of the three frameworks projects described in Chapter 10 will show that differing interpretations at each stage will produce different strings of modules. It is only during planning stages for a course, however, that the content of each module retains its place in the string. Earlier (p. 100) I referred to linking units together, as though they were beads on a string. This is done by teachers for the sake of having plans for their courses. Once classroom interaction begins, however, and the content of all the units is introduced (by the teacher according to plan, or on request from learners at various times), a better image for what happens is that of certain molecular structures, where molecules are in constant motion, yet linked up with one another to form a distinctive substance (see p. 142 for an example).

The concrete illustrations which I have given are from case studies that happened to involve adult learners only. However, there is no reason why, if the general principles of design are adhered to and the stages of implementation followed, frameworks cannot also be produced for teaching children and adolescents. (An approach to needs surveys for children, and ways of obtaining their input into course design, will be introduced later.)

Setting up a course

Learner involvement

A needs survey has to be carried out before frameworks are written in the first place, but more information is often required before a particular course derived from a set of frameworks can be prepared. It is this second-level needs survey that is being examined here. Presumably something will already be known about the characteristics of learners who will be taking the courses in question, also about their language needs in a general way. A teacher will need to get more detailed, more specific information about the learners in order to have their input when selecting the modules to be used as well as in choosing and preparing classroom activities.

What information should be sought, and how? Three categories are most commonly used.

1. General background information as well as information about educational level, previous language learning experience, and current proficiency in the target language. In many instances the latter kind of information is available, but not biographies. Yet biographies are often useful in discovering what topics and situations will be of interest (and not only of use) to learners.
2. Language needs. Most frequently, the overall purpose for the course is known (job-specific, or general education, or for daily life, for example). At this stage more information on situations of use and a breakdown of topics and language skills most needed will be invaluable.
3. Learning styles and preferences. As long as teachers do not believe in imposing a standard approach to learning (and one would hope that they would not), it is not only reasonable but also necessary to collect this kind of information.

Collecting information is not necessarily an onerous task. Much has been written on formal approaches to needs surveys, involving large projects and very detailed analysis of the data (see, e.g., Jupp and Hodlin 1975; Mackay and Mountford 1978; Richterich and Chancerel 1980; Hoedt 1981; Freudenstein, Beneke, and Pönisch 1981; Schutz and Derwing 1981). In some situations this is both desirable and possible. In others, it is neither. There may be neither time nor resources to undertake a formal survey, and there may be no support for the idea. But teachers working on their own or with each other can use a variety of techniques thiat involve little or no expense and are not bothersome or threatening to the learners. Before using any of them, it is well to sketch out what one's objectives are; then as information becomes available, the needs analysis can be rounded out and completed. The amount and kind of background information *already available* can be determined, and further items added to the list. A simple checklist of purposes, situations, and topics can be drawn up (and later expanded *ad infinitum*). Items concerning attitudes and learning styles can also be added to the stock of questions to be answered as the course progresses. (See Yalden 1983: 162–76 for sample checklists, and see Rubin and Thompson 1982 for items on attitudes and learning styles.)

To gather the information, the teacher can use

– observation
– discussion and negotiation
– questionnaires
– interviews.

In addition, it is possible to get the learners to do some of the analysis independently. I will discuss each of these approaches in turn.

Observation scarcely requires any explanation. If a checklist or a set of notes is at hand, a teacher can begin to fill in the blanks, as it were, from the very first moment the class begins. Soon a quantity of information about the learners, organized in a purposeful way, will emerge.

Discussion and negotiation will also be more fruitful if the teacher's purposes have been thought through beforehand. There is nothing wrong with simply asking the learners quite directly who they are and what they are interested in – if there is a common language of communication. If not, other techniques have to be used. Sometimes, even if the teacher and the learners share a common language, the result of discussion may seem to be a hopelessly wide range of interests and wants. An excellent solution in some situations is a negotiated approach, in which the learners are made to choose from among the needs of the whole class. In one variation, *ad hoc* analysis, students are asked to rank-order a list of objectives (either teacher prepared, or gathered through some form of needs survey from the learners themselves). Further rank ordering takes place in small groups, and the class as a whole has to negotiate the final rank order. The list might be of topics (airport, taxis, restaurants, hotels, sight-seeing, etc.) or of tasks (making a phone call, buying a car, going to the dentist, getting a watch fixed, negotiating a contract) or of language skills (understanding English grammar better, learning more vocabulary, writing exams, taking clear lecture notes). This kind of analysis also involves the students very directly in determining the main focus of the course (Shaw 1982).

Questionnaires have received quite a lot of attention, and many examples have been published (see for example, Mackay 1978; Mackay and Bosquet 1981). Included here are a set of guidelines that can be used for questionnaire construction. The extract is from the *Teachers' Handbook for the Frameworks for Communication Needs Courses, Survival and General Purposes* (Fitzgerald and Pagurek 1984a: 20). It illustrates as well the methodological bias of the project.

Getting to Know the Learners.
In order to develop a course which meets the learners' communication needs in your language, it will be necessary for you to find out more about the people in your class. Use the first few classes (while you are teaching the "preliminaries") to get to know more about the learners' backgrounds, learning styles and language needs. Depending on the preferences of both you and your class, you can obtain this information by observation, discussion or written questionnaire. Here are some questions to ask and topics to consider.
a) Background. Biographical information plus educational level, previous language learning experience and current proficiency in the target language.
b) Learning styles. You can ask learners questions such as the following:
  – Do you learn better through the ear, the eye, or the ear and eye together?
  – Do you prefer to learn by trial and error, or by imitation?
  – Do you prefer to master each step completely before going on to something new, or do you prefer to have exposure to many new things without completely mastering all of them, knowing you will come back to them later?
  – Do you think learning happens only in the classroom?
  – Who should decide what you learn: you? the teacher? you and the teacher together?
  – Can you learn only from your teacher or from fellow students also?
  – Do you think it is important to learn the grammatical rules of a language before trying to speak it?
  – Do you mind making mistakes in the target language when you are in the classroom? when you are talking to native speakers?
c) Language needs.
  – Why are you learning this language? (business, pleasure, etc.)
  – Will you need to write/read/speak/listen in the language?
  – In what situations will you use the language? (shopping? at the bank? at the workplace?)
While gathering input from the learners about their perception of their language needs, you are viewing these needs in relation to the reality of your culture, in order to modify or supplement as necessary.

Here is a questionnaire written by a teacher of Dutch who used the situation-based frameworks for an evening class for adults. She knew little about the learners who had registered. The questionnaire was used in the first hour of class, and in subsequent classes as a basis for discussion of their purposes and learning styles.

Dutch 1
Instructor: Ingrid Berljawsky

133

All information is voluntary and will be kept strictly confidential.

Background
Name:
Telephone:
Age:
Education:
Occupation:
Language skills
Native language:
Language spoken at home:
What other languages can you
– understand
– speak
– read
– write
(please indicate whether fluently, well or in a limited way)

Course
Why are you taking this course?
Which language skills will you need and how important are they to you:
– comprehension
– speech
– reading
– writing
In what situation(s) will you use Dutch (e.g. socially, traveling, reading)?

Learning style
How important is it to you to learn the grammatical rules?
Do you like group work? Why or why not?
How do you feel about making mistakes while learning a new language?
What do you think the role of the teacher is in second-language teaching?

Comments
Anything else you'd like to add?

The questionnaire is a relatively economical way of gathering helpful information. A few precautions, however, are in order. Some learners will be quite used to filling out questionnaires and not be troubled by the idea at all. Others may feel distinctly threatened by what they may perceive as an attempt to pry into their personal lives. Still others may interpret the use of a questionnaire as an admission of lack of professional knowledge on the teacher's part ("Why are you asking me how I want to learn a language? Don't you know how a language should be learned?"). Tact is therefore required. It is not, for example, advisable to mail out questionnaires that the learners do not know are coming. Nor is it a good idea to pass them out in class without any explanation of what they are for, and without making sure the class has understood. Learners have been reduced to tears by teachers who seem autocratic, even if it is the last thing intended. (On one occasion a learner thought the questionnaire was a test, and suffered agonies trying to give the "right" answers to the questions.) Furthermore, the language in which the questionnaire is written should be at a level that the learners can understand – not as obvious a suggestion as it might be.

Interviews represent a further procedure that has often been used. Not only the learners, but also other teachers, administrators, parents, employers, or sponsors can provide helpful information at times. It is best to structure them somewhat, in the interests of economy – that is, to make a checklist of items of information that one hopes to gather during the interview. Often unexpected or surprising information also turns up, so it is best to keep an open mind and to allow the interviewee to talk freely, at least as much as time permits. Part of a checklist used in the preparation of the "Frameworks for Communication Needs Courses, Intermediate Level" (Yalden and Bosquet 1984b) is reproduced here as an illustration of the structured interview. It is only one part of a much longer set of notes for the interviewers. The interviewers studied the list and kept it by them as they talked to the commercial officers who represented the future group of learners. At the end, a learner profile was drawn up from the information gathered in this way.

Part C. Communication Needs

C–1   Interactional needs
The purpose of Section C–1 is to obtain in raw data form an inventory of target tasks, i.e., those tasks identified as required in order for a commercial officer to function adequately in a particular target situation and in a particular target domain.
   C–1–a   Elicit all settings where target language is used in target situations. Enter information in appropriate category, i.e Worklife/social life/domestic life.
   C–1–b   Elicit information on interlocutors dealt with and roles played by officers in target situations. Enter information in appropriate categories as above.
   C–1–c   Elicit what officers do in an average day in the target language in host country. Enter information.
   C–1–d   Elicit information about tasks and topics dealt with, and enter information. Use questions such as: If you were requesting and imparting information in target language what topics would you be dealing with? (Note: it might be necessary to explain and refine the reference to the function 'requesting and imparting information')
   C–1–e   Elicit information on frequency of use. Use questions like: How often in your work life, etc., would you use the target language?
(Yalden and Bosquet 1984b: II, 5)

Sets of notes such as these may be written in any way the teacher thinks best, as long as the categories correspond to the categories of information he has set out to gather.

Independent needs analysis for adults or for children is independent in that the learner carries out tasks that have been prepared by the teacher. For adults, the tasks can be easily related to the purposes for which the target language is being learned, and are essentially a kind of fieldwork. They can be done individually or in groups. A group of ESL university-preparatory students might, for example, be asked to (a) observe a certain class or attend a lecture, (b) view a related videotape, (c) examine past test or examination papers for the subject, (d) talk to one of the students in the class (using a structured format), (e) find what the homework or assignments are like for the course. The object of all of this might be to find out what the workload for the course is and whether the student feels ready to begin it. Similar field trips can be arranged for groups of immigrant learners. Presumably professionals could make their own arrangements to get information. High school age students could be given tasks related to their personal interests, or to a theme selected by the group – in such cases the line between needs survey and interaction activities in the target language is fine indeed, and the feedback to the teacher very rapid.

For young children, home and school life are all-important. A technique for finding out in what roles and situations a target language is used outside the classroom, what topics come up, and when the children would *like* to be able to use the target language involves a drawing activity. In one project carried out in a multilingual situation,[1] the children were asked to write their name, age, country of birth, and all languages spoken at home (first, second, third...) on a sheet (Table 11.1 presents a summary of the data from one class). Next, each of them was asked to draw a stick figure representing him- or herself. Then they were asked to draw boxes around the figure, and in the boxes, to enter the answers for three questions for each situation of target language use or contact:

– Where were you?
– Who were you with?
– Why were you speaking English?

Locations that emerged included home, neighborhood, street, park, store, schoolyard. Mediums included TV, movies, books, telephone. The responses to the questions *where* and *with whom* were easily analyzed, but the *why* posed greater problems, since a good many categories emerged – for example, for information, for fun, because the person did not speak French.

1 Julia Carey designed and executed the needs survey described. The classes, given at the Lycée Claudel in Ottawa, were linguistically mixed: the children's first languages were either French, English or one of a number of other tongues. Some of the classes were designed as English first language, some as English second language, depending on the characteristics of the children in them. The children were between 9 and 14 years of age.

TABLE 11.1 CHARACTERISTICS OF THE CHILDREN WHOSE WANTS ARE SHOWN IN
FIGURE 11.1

Age range
9½ to 12 years

Countries of origin

Algeria	Holland	Mauritius
Belgium	Hungary	Poland
Canada	India	Senegal
France	Ireland	Sweden
Haiti	Jamaica	United States

Language(s) spoken at home
French – 7
English – 5
French and English – 13
French, English, and Spanish – 1

Dominant language
French – 50%
English – 50%

A master sheet was prepared for each class, showing all of the information compiled (see Figure 11.1). The data were exploited in a variety of ways. They showed the students how they used the language, and that it was not just a school subject. The data were used as a research tool, for example, to indicate the range of contact with the target language and the recurring areas of use (e.g., most of the children watched TV). They helped to identify the kind of language children learned outside of class and, most important, helped the teacher to see what kind of English was useful and appropriate to help them function in their own world. The data also assisted the teacher in choosing material, making it possible to tune in to existing patterns and interests, and bridge the gap between existing experience and new areas the children had not explored. One of the results was that the children themselves made suggestions: that they be taken on field trips where they would have to use English, that they all go to a movie together, and so on.

It is true that the setting for this particular project was one that favors the acquisition of the target language (English) to a very high degree, but the overall approach to learning about the learners and getting them involved in the language course is applicable to many other situations. (It also produces some delightful drawings and unexpected language needs, such as English for schoolyard fights.)

A similar procedure might be used with learners whose literacy skills were weak, and of course, instead of stick figures, the information can

Home	Computers	Camp
family	Asking	counselors
guests	Answering	campers

Lessons
ballet
piano
swimming
coach/teacher

School
recess
friends
play

Dentist

Games
Dungeons & Dragons

Sports
Spectators
Coach
Players

Neighborhood
park
street
back yard

Store
salesperson

Books
newspapers
magazines

Television
"Different Strokes"
"Happy Days"
cartoons
"Mash"
etc.

Street
bus stop
on bus
friends/strangers

Self
reflection
working out
    problems

Figure 11.1 Situations and role sets for 27 children.

be entered using a grid to show interlocutors and topics or any other combination of categories for which the teacher wants to get information (Table 11.2). All of this information could be fed back into the description of purpose for the course, and into the description of proficiency or of communicative competence being used (see Chapter 2).

Selecting units

As the needs survey proceeds, the teacher will form an idea of what kind of focus to give to the course, and will need to choose the appropriate units from the frameworks and arrange them for pedagogical treatment. The teacher consults the complete set of frameworks, makes a selection, and then uses the units to develop corresponding target language units. Furthermore, once teachers become accustomed to developing target language units from existing frameworks, they will have no trouble writing similar units to cover

TABLE 11.2 TRACKING GRID I: ROLE SETS AND TOPICS

Interlocutors[a]	Personal identification	House and home	Trade, profession, occupation	Free-time entertainment	Travel	Relations with other people	Health and welfare	Education	Shopping	Food and drink	Services	Places	Languages	Weather
Stranger														
Policeman														
Teacher														
Doctor														
Employer														
Neighbor														
Friend														
Etc.														

Note: A checkmark is placed in the square to indicate what topics might be talked about with which interlocutors. Similar grids may be used for the written mode. The range of topics along the top is that given in Threshold Level. Each is broken down quite finely; for each topic, a separate grid can be made.

[a] Interlocutors can be specified for a group of students, or a grid may be filled out for each learner individually.

Source: Yalden (1983).

additional situations or tasks. (See pp. 143 and 147.) To illustrate this process, let us suppose that the prototypical units available are the ones that were prepared for the CNCs for survival and general purposes, together with those for the commercial officers, to wit:

a) *Situation-based frameworks*

Setting off on a trip	At the bank
At the airport	At the post office
Local transportation	At a government office
Shopping for food	At someone's house
Shopping for other items	In an emergency
Eating in a restaurant	Planning a journey
Finding accommodation	etc.

b) *Task-based frameworks*

Monitoring	Introducing business people to
Reading for information	government officials
Using the telephone	Answering inquiries
Gathering information	Negotiating agreements
Making inquiries	

There are many possible combinations, assembled according to the needs of the learners, time available, and so on. There are in addition, in these frameworks, the preliminary units on notions, social skills, and management of discourse. A selection from all of the units available can be made in such a way as to provide a course specific to the goals of the learners, whether these be tourism, a particular kind of work, a research trip to East Africa, a tour of duty in Japan, and so on. (The addition of other units makes possible the extension of the list of possible course objectives, as desired.) It will be remembered that there is no sequencing implied in the frameworks, and that cyclical use is recommended.

For beginners, the strongest unit is the one on social skills, which will "anchor" the learner in the language. That is, it has the important function of allowing a learner to express his own identity and learn the identity of others.[2] A unit on phonology would also be needed. Thus, for a short preliminary or beginning course, the pattern shown in Figure 11.3 would be suitable. If the learners wanted to concentrate on language to be used on arrival in another country, a purely situational string might be used, as shown in Figure 11.4. If the learners were absolute beginners, but were anxious to get some situational vocabulary and expressions started, the teacher might plan to use the combination shown in Figure 11.5. Yet another possibility mixes in preliminaries, situations, and tasks (see Figure 11.6).

2 George Chouchani provided this description of "anchoring" at the time the situation-based frameworks were being first discussed, and the other teachers in the project readily concur.

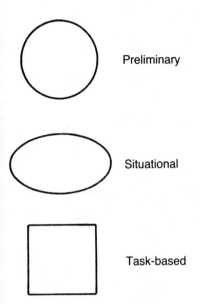

Preliminary

Situational

Task-based

Figure 11.2 Types of units.

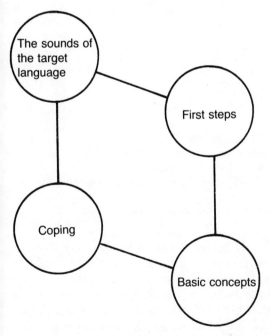

Figure 11.3 Pattern for preliminary activities in a second language course.

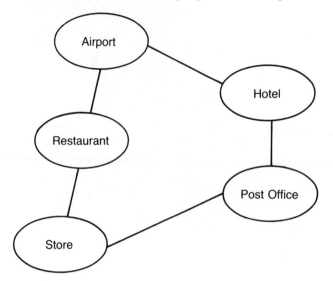

Figure 11.4 A situational string.

A course outline produced by a teacher using the situation-based frameworks is shown below. Although the units are presented as a list, they were used to form the molecular structure described earlier – that is, once they were all introduced, they bounced around, collided with each other, were in constant motion.

A. Introduction to Dutch
1. Coping
2. First steps toward communication
3. Expressing basic concepts

Dealing with situations
1. What's that sign – road signs, public notices
2. Getting around – getting information, using trains and buses
3. Shopping – getting information, making purchases
4. Using the telephone – making and accepting calls, making appointments, getting information
5. Eating out – ordering food and drink, consulting the staff

The possibilities are limited only by the needs of the learners and the teacher's imagination. The variations in arrangement can be made as the course progresses – it is not necessary to have the entire structure in place before the course begins. In fact, more often than not, the teacher will need to transpose the units little by little, because of practical constraints. If it is possible or desirable to get an overview of the entire course, by selecting and transposing the objectives and transaction-type

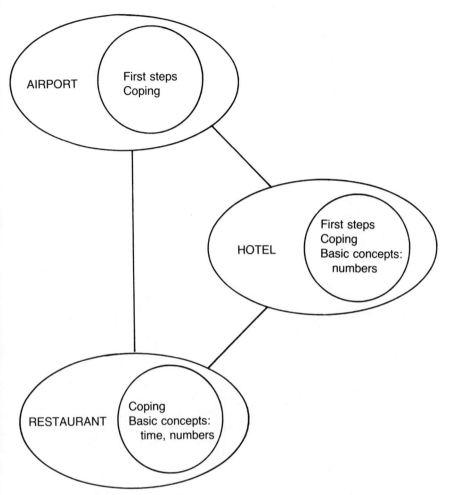

Figure 11.5 Preliminaries within situational units.

units into the target language, the teacher will know in advance the scope of the work – vocabulary, grammar, functions. The overview might help in decisions about sequencing linguistic items. The classroom activities could be selected afterward.

Preparing for the classroom

Transposition

Once the prototypical units have been chosen (for all or part of the course), teachers next have to *transpose* (not translate) them both lin-

143

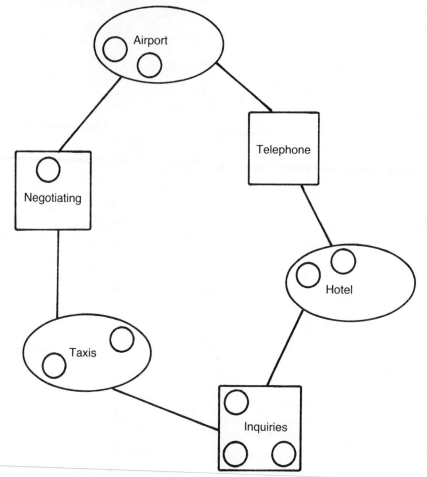

Figure 11.6 A mixed string. (Small circles represent preliminaries.)

guistically and culturally into the situation for which they are designing their course. This is a central principle. If teachers take a framework and attempt merely to translate the English words, phrases, and structures, they may come up with something that is either nonsensical or useless or both. To accomplish a transposition, teachers must ask themselves questions about the target language and the target situation in which it is to be used. A teacher might, for example, be asked to do the following:

Think out some activities for a unit on telephone numbers and addresses. The objectives are that the students will be able to ask for and give phone numbers, ask for and give other types of identification, ask for and give addresses, and count from one to whatever number you decide on. The framework suggests that vocabulary items will be needed in certain categories, and examples in English are provided.

The teacher of a particular target language will have to look at these instructions and think, "Is it in fact necessary to know how to give and ask for phone numbers on Mars? They don't have phones there; all messages are carried by laser beams. I'll scratch this objective. What about identification? Well, they don't use identity cards, but on every street corner you may be asked for your social insurance number. You'd better be able to give that. Apartment numbers . . . they don't have any, only houses and they aren't numbered, so forget that. Bank accounts . . . yes, everyone has at least six, so we have to have some work on those." And so on. For each language, each culture, the teacher will have to take a given framework prototypical unit and think, "What is the cultural information, the linguistic information, the social information, that learners need before they can proceed?"

Most teachers can do this quite rapidly, and speed increases as familiarity with the concept grows. In the frameworks projects already completed, the transposing process has been helpful to some teachers who had not been in the habit of questioning the usefulness to learners of the activities provided. Initial concentration on content at a semantic rather than a formal level provides a good deal of freedom to develop a lesson, while still giving the teacher something to start with. Depending on a teacher's background and familiarity with the purposes of the learners, the derivation of the target language unit from the prototype may proceed intuitively, or it might be necessary to consult authentic samples of the target language for the necessary sociolinguistic information, before going on to selection of language forms and preparation of classroom materials.

Note also that if a framework being used includes a section on useful words and expressions, it cannot usually cover all the useful words connected with a given concept. When choosing words and expressions in the target language, it is useful to remember the following two points:

1. When there are different ways of saying something, there are often one or two expressions that are easier to cope with, either because they are short, simple, or easy to pronounce (e.g., "Coffee, please," rather than "Do you think I might have some coffee?").
2. Nevertheless, some expressions, though not necessarily "easy," are particularly valuable, because they can be used for a variety of purposes and in a variety of situations. In English, for example, "Excuse me" – to apologize, to get attention, to interrupt, and so on – and "thing" – for general reference – are both useful, but not necessarily easy to pronounce. It is up

to the teacher to make appropriate selections for the class he is designing. (See Fitzgerald and Pagurek 1984a: 27.)

A final point on transposition: It is sometimes useful to consult the learners themselves on whether the *objectives* in a unit seem sensible to them before proceeding – occasionally learners will reject, if not the whole unit, some of the objectives specified in it.

TRANSPOSITION EXAMPLES FROM FIRST STEPS TOWARD COMMUNICATION

(one of the Carleton frameworks: see Appendix B)

1. Cultural considerations: extract from the framework
   - Are people formal/informal when they address/introduce other people?
   - What body language should you be aware of (e.g., shaking hands – is this appropriate/acceptable?)
   - Do people stand close to/far from each other when speaking?
   - What topics are considered acceptable/taboo when first meeting people? (e.g., religion, marital status) (Fitzgerald and Pagurek 1984b: 2)

2. Transposition: cultural questions for discussion (extract from course in Arabic worked up by G. Chouchani)
   - Men introduce other men, their wives
   - Women introduce other women or wait to be introduced by their husbands
   - Formal introductions involve shaking hands (strong handshake for men, soft handshake for women)
   - Bowing the head slightly when introduced
   - Use of titles in appropriate situations (formal)
   - Use of surname and title (formal)
   - Use of first name (informal)
   - Use of vocative /ya/ (informal) – for example, ya John (Oh John)
   - Telephone numbers, hotel room numbers required when arranging appointments.

3. Objective (a) from *First Steps Toward Communication*
   - Introductions and Nationality

Transactions	Useful words/expressions
Introduce oneself and say where one is from/one's nationality	I'm (name). My name is....
	I'd like to introduce myself. I don't think we've met. I come from...
Understand questions about origins/nationality	Where are you from?
	Are you (nationality)?

   (Fitzgerald and Pagurek 1984b: 4)

4. Transposition: introductions – from G. Chouchani's notes for a course in Arabic

- Introducing oneself/one's nationality with introduction of pronominal suffixes, for example:

ism i – may name   /ism/ = name
ism ak – your (masc.) name
ism ik – your (fem.) name
ism u – his name
ism aha – her name

Grammar note: There is no verb "to be" in the present/imperfect tense; therefore expressions translate literally into "I John," not "I am John."

- Introduction of nationality adjectives (e.g., Canadian, from Canada)
Word list – names places (cities in Egypt, countries)
List of appropriate expressions for Egyptian Arabic

Even in preparing a simple introductory unit on introductions in Arabic, cultural and linguistic differences show up clearly. However, the teacher of Dutch in making a transposition of the prototypical unit called *Coping* (see Appendix B, p. 184, which lists cultural considerations like "How do target language speakers view attempts to speak their language?" and "How do target language speakers help nonspeakers to understand – by talking more loudly and deliberately, like English speakers?") decided not to devote any special attention to cultural considerations at all, since there are relatively few differences between Dutch and Canadian customs. As a result, what minor differences there are were dealt with as they arose. The objectives, on the other hand, were relevant, and so the teacher passed directly to those.

On further inspection of the transactions provided in the framework called *Coping*, the teacher decided that one of them was not useful, and so omitted it. It was "Understand an offer to get someone who speaks English." She added instead, "State ability to speak English only or other languages." In the section on "Getting the native speaker to help you," the same teacher added a transaction that was not in the framework: "Ask someone to write something down." Each teacher has to make the adjustments he feels is needed to suit the particular group of learners for whom the course is being prepared. The adjustments may come from the nature of the target language or culture, or they may spring from the needs survey.

Selection and adjustment of teaching and learning activities will be discussed shortly.

Creating new units

If there is no prototypical unit for a situation the teacher and the learners want to cover, the teacher can create one of his own. The steps to be followed are the same ones that materials writers follow when drawing up prototypical units. Creating new units, once a teacher is accustomed

147

to the notion of prototypes, and understands how these were written, is not a difficult matter. Here is a procedure suggested to teachers using the situation-based frameworks.

Step 1: Decide on the situation (e.g., At the Doctor's Office)
Step 2: Think about the situation as it is experienced in the target culture. Make a list of what people have to do in this situation. (e.g., Make an appointment, tell the nurse you are there, describe symptoms, etc.). This constitutes a list of communication objectives.
Step 3: Think about the transactions which occur in the process of achieving each objective – for example:

Objective	*Transactions*
Making an appointment	Calling the doctor's office
	Stating the purpose of the call
	Arranging a time
	Changing a time

Step 4: Write down words and expression needed to negotiate each transaction:

Transaction	*Language (English example)*
Calling the office	Good morning.
	Dr. X's office.
	This is (name).

Step 5: Consider the language selected in Step 4, from the point of view of grammar, vocabulary, pronunciation, etc. Prepare the teaching material.
Step 6: Create listening activities. Write dialogues which focus on one or two of the transactions using the language from your list. Draw or find pictures which will provide the context for each dialogue. Record the dialogues on tape.
Step 7: Find or create activities which will allow learners to practice the transaction for each objective.

(Fitzgerald and Pagurek 1984b: 23–5)

Each framework will have a somewhat different form, but the general principles are the same – movement from a situation of language use or a task to be accomplished verbally to the language tokens that the learners need to carry forward their own purposes.

Selecting activities

Although the choice of activities used in a frameworks-based course can be very wide indeed, there are a number of assumptions underlying their selection and indeed the whole notion of the frameworks. Most of these have been made clear in Parts II and III, but since this work is concerned primarily with an approach to course design that takes semantic content of interactions as its starting point, not much has been said about particular teaching techniques. In fact, it is not my intention to go into the question of techniques and activities in great detail – that would be the subject of a book on methodology, not on course design. However, the topic of teaching techniques and how to choose them does indeed require some treatment here, since it is crucial to the implementation of the frameworks in a particular teaching situation.

In order to move to this discussion, some fundamental issues have to be considered.

BASIC ASSUMPTIONS

Second language acquisition and first language acquisition processes are similar in many important aspects, but they also differ in many ways. Much of the research that supported the hypothesis that they are the same is now being reconsidered (see, e.g., the discussion in Davies et al. 1984, and especially Long and Sato in that volume), and the differences between the two processes are once again receiving considerable attention. What the effect of formal instruction is and what its content should be are two questions that of course are of considerable concern to the classroom teacher. Recent studies (Long 1983a) confirm the usefulness of classroom work, although there is still lively debate over what *kind* of work is best. The work on the differences in the processes necessarily divides into two categories: work on children and work on adults (I include adolescents in the adult category). An important point of disagreement among teachers and researchers is generally the question of grammar: What role does it play in second language development? How should it be taught, if at all? and so on. For example, one reads, in a discussion of the shift of emphasis in second language acquisition research away from an analysis of linguistic structures alone toward the process of learning:

The learning of a language must be viewed as a very complex process of which the development of a grammatical system is only one part; properties (syntactic, phonological, etc.) of L1 and L2 certainly do have some influence on this process and may account for *some* aspects of the learner's interlanguage. But again: other factors, especially psychological ones, are likely to be of much greater importance for our understanding of the process of L2 acquisition, including linguistic and non-linguistic strategies involved. (Meisel, Clahsen, and Pienemann 1981: 110)

The learning of a language, whether first or second, is certainly viewed now as being very complex. The question is whether it is entirely a natural process, and if it is, whether it is possible to identify and describe the stages. The position taken throughout this work is that second language development is a natural process (which nevertheless shows variation from one individual to another), and that it can be helped by teaching. Teaching serves to speed up the process of moving from one

149

stage of interlanguage to another, and of moving one element of an interlanguage closer to the target language (Meisel et al. 1981). There are, however, constraints on what can be taught effectively and when. Pienemann's research with child learners suggests that there are certain psychological constraints on language teachability, which means that a structure can be learned under instruction only if the learner's interlanguage has already reached a stage one step before the acquisition of the structure to be taught. This does not mean, however, that teaching has to replicate the natural process – even if it were known exactly what that is. And it does not mean giving up formal instruction of syntax, since the problem of fossilization in interlanguage is a very real one (whether the learners are children or adults), and it has to be dealt with.

> Giving up the instruction of syntax is to allow for the fossilization of inter-languages in a simplified form. . . . Such a fossilization often appears with the natural L2 acquisition in minority groups. . . . Of course, it is unclear whether fossilization can be avoided by instruction, but abandoning the instruction of syntax at this point in time is not to care about how this question can be solved. (Pienemann 1984: 209)

The assumption that adult learners can reactivate the language acquisition capacity that they had as children presents further problems:

> I have several problems with this view [of reactivation]. One is that of fossilization. . . . The second reservation involves the considerable individual differences one finds in SLA. There is such clear evidence of differential success in L2 (compared to L1) – which I feel might override surface similarities – that I feel one must come to the conclusion (if one holds a universal-grammar point of view) that adult learners reactivate latent capacities differentially and one wonders why this should be so. (Selinker 1984: 336)

The big difference between the first and second language acquisition processes is the presence or absence of the first language itself. The presence of a first language means that the learner will tend to compare its linguistic forms as well as its rhetorical structure to those of the second, and to draw conclusions that may or may not be correct or useful. Furthermore, the learner will have acquired strategies for communicating and for manipulating language that may or may not be appropriate when applied to second language situations of use.

Since much second language acquisition goes on in classroom situations, teachers are often involved. They intervene in the process by setting up activities, choosing drills and exercises, and so on – that is, in lesson planning and in teaching. The frameworks take them a good part of the way, but not to the point of having lesson plans ready-made for them. How can they plan their interventions? What techniques will best preserve the proportional quality of the underlying syllabus design? How should they deal with the problem of syntax? There are several criteria for arranging classroom instruction that, if applied, will guide the teacher in making choices. These are described in the next section, and are followed by examples from the situation-based frameworks.

CRITERIA FOR CHOICE

Although the purpose of using frameworks to design courses is to encourage an interactive, communicative approach to second language study, no barriers to overt study of grammar and vocabulary are implied. To this end, a variety of drills may be used, and the choice depends on learner preference and availability of teaching materials, as well as the teacher's own bias. The questions of whether drills are effective, and if so, what kinds are most effective have been treated in the many thousands of pages that have been written on the virtues of one method as opposed to another. It is not my purpose to discuss this matter again; teachers continue to have their own preferences, as do experienced learners, and choices will continue to be made from what is available or what remains to be invented. (One wonders if it is possible to add anything to the enormous stocks available, but the resourcefulness of teachers is continually surprising.)

It is, however, assumed that a minimum of time will be spent on structural activities in a frameworks-based course, and furthermore that if students want or need to work directly on the structures of the target language, that they will do so primarily on their own time. Much depends on the learners themselves, too. It may be that they will not have had much opportunity to study languages previously, and so would need a teacher's guidance to approach structural drills and exercises, even if they are encouraged to do these on their own time. Other learners may not want to spend much time on homework assignments (especially if they are busy professionals), and so structural work may need to be undertaken during class hours. But the purpose of much language learning that goes on today is such that structural work cannot form the only basis for a course. Learners require opportunities to communicate in the target language, and the frameworks are used to prepare such opportunities.

The kinds of activities that should be stressed are the ones known now as "communicative," "interactive," "task-oriented." Sample materials from existing sets of frameworks serve to illustrate this assumption. The focus of the activities should be on meanings to be communicated, and not on forms and structures to be learned. There is now a significant number of reference works that can assist teachers to write their own activities (see, e.g., Grellet 1981; Littlewood 1981). There are also many textbooks for ESL and other languages that can be used directly or as sources of inspiration. Generally speaking, in

151

looking for or writing suitable activities, Littlewood's criteria (1981: 17–18) should be followed: Activities should provide "whole-task" practice, improve motivation, allow natural learning, and create a context that supports learning. Some of the activities that were recognized some years ago as meeting many of these criteria are role plays and other drama techniques, simulations, problem-solving tasks, and information-transfer and information-gap activities. Interactive tasks of all kinds carried out by groups of learners have also been strongly recommended. These range from simple activities like building constructions from a few index cards and paper clips to much more elaborate group projects like researching and writing a report on whether a university should or should not continue to receive funding for one of its programs (Cumming 1984). For the sample materials derived from the situation-based frameworks, teachers were advised to follow these guidelines:

1. A task should be realistic; it should be something the learner will do in the target language.
2. Whenever possible, there should be an information gap: A learner should have information that other learners (or the teacher) do not have but need in order to complete the task.
3. Depending on the level of the class, the activity can allow for freedom of choice for the speaker (in terms of the forms of the language *and* the meaning to be expressed), which produces a high degree of unpredictable language for the hearer. Neither the language nor the sequence of ideas is specified in advance, and so the learners are free to use whatever language they have at their disposal to perform the task at hand (Fitzgerald and Pagurek 1984a).

Since activities must be chosen in terms of the topics, situations, and tasks that have been identified as most useful for a given group of learners, it is impossible to specify in advance what they will be. Teachers should accustom themselves to searching for ideas in order to assemble their own resource kits or bundles of activities. (See the next section for further discussion.) What is essential for the learner is a flexible approach to combining structural practice (preferably solitary) with interactive, communicative tasks (with the teacher, in groups, using a computer). The latter type of activity should predominate, although at certain times during a course or sequence of courses the former may be more heavily weighted. Group work, although it involves nonnative speakers of the target language, is proving to be very effective in second language acquisition, with no evidence of incorrect forms of the target language appearing as a result of it (Long and Porter 1985). It is most necessary to incorporate it into classroom work for most of the activity types recommended here.

A final note. Grammar can be taught communicatively by being presented in a context. It is not necessary, therefore, to think in terms of syntax being taught solely by drills. A grammatical item can be presented by the teacher, using expressions from a unit being currently taught. It can then be incorporated into communicative activities. For example, to teach Yes/No questions in a unit on ordering meals in a restaurant, sentences like the following could be presented:

Aux	*Subject*	*Base form*	*Predicate*
Do	we	need	a reservation
	you	take	credit cards
		have	a non-smoking area
		serve	(food item)

Then the practice of Yes/No questions could be integrated into an activity aimed at finding out about restaurants:

Learners work in pairs.
A has information about various restaurants, and takes the role of restaurant owner.
B has a chart to fill in showing facilities, foods, etc., for different restaurants.
B asks A questions using the structure to be practiced, e.g., "Do you have music?"
A replies according to the information he holds.
B fills in the chart accordingly.

One can imagine the same technique being applied to a large number of types of content: for children, TV programs; for commercial transactions, types of industrial or agricultural equipment; for political officials, election results; and so on.

The same is true of most of the sample materials included here. The underlying aim of the activity is what is important in building up a repertoire of teaching techniques. The content can be adapted to the needs of the moment. So one works in two directions at once: from the content, based on a needs survey, toward the appropriate techniques, and from a bank or repertoire of techniques or activities toward the appropriate content.

Activities banks

Teachers using frameworks need to build up their own repertoire of techniques. These should include structural teaching techniques as well

153

as techniques that focus on meaning. There is an immense literature to choose from, and it can be somewhat confusing. But if categories are established in advance, the search can be rewarding. Here are some categories for a basic bookshelf:[3]

Reference grammars (teachers' and learners')
Works in the theoretical foundations of language teaching
General works on methodology
Practical works on various aspects or facets of language teaching, and sources of classroom material.

The last is the largest category, and includes textbooks and journals as well as collections of ideas and activities.

From a collection started along these lines, and from any other sources available, the teacher should build up a resource kit of activity types. There are various approaches to doing this, which essentially involve creating filing systems of all kinds. A teacher might keep role plays on index cards; information-gap exercises or activities can also be kept on index cards, with one color for player A, one for player B, and so on. A sample activity can be given a cover sheet indicating what level it is for, what language items it focuses on (if any), what language functions are stressed, what kinds of interactions are involved. Then similar activities can be filed with it as they are discovered. Grids can be prepared to categorize activity types (Table 11.3). The possibilities are endless, and limited only by the imagination of the teacher.

Since a project of this kind can grow very large indeed, it is often useful for groups of teachers to cooperate in setting up small resource centers. One of these has consisted of nothing more than a small cart with two shelves, filled with cardboard boxes containing materials of various sorts. It was wheeled from one classroom to another, depending on which teacher wanted to use it. It also turned into a resource that the learners could use on their own. Other such centers are usually housed in cupboards or small rooms – a surprising amount of material can fit into a small space. If several teachers work together on setting up a resource center, the ideas generated are usually impressive, and the rewards great for all concerned.

Taking the idea a step further, it is possible also to set up activities banks or resource centers for groups of institutions to use. If resources are available, there is much to be said for a community center of some sort. A final extension of the activity bank is to set up a center for self-directed learning that the learners themselves can use – and help to stock

3 The "basic bookshelf" idea goes back to versions of a "bare-bones" bibliography for TESL, submitted by several experts to the December 1979 issue of the *TESOL Newsletter*. An adaptation for English and French as second languages can be found in Mollica and Yalden (1984: 117–19).

TABLE 11.3 TRACKING GRID 2: COMBINING EXERCISES (OR EXERCISE TYPES) AND RHETORICAL, DISCOURSE, AND STUDY SKILLS (THIS EXAMPLE PROVIDES A MIXED SELECTION)

Exercises (or Types)[a]	Unit 1: Skimming & scanning	Unit 2: Recording information	Unit 3: Organizing information	Unit 4: Extracting salient points to summarize	Unit 5: Expanding relevant points into a summary
E_1					
E_2					
E_3					
E_4					
E_5 etc.					

Note: Place a checkmark in the appropriate cells and/or use the squares to record relevant classroom materials.
[a] Exercise types could be listed for oral and/or written discourse (e.g., role play, simulation, games, problem solving).
Source: Yalden (1983).

and run. This approach is full of promise, and fits well with the inter-active approach to second language course design advocated in this work.

Such activities banks are excellent ways of stocking authentic materials of all sorts. (It should be clear that both scripted and authentic materials can be used in frameworks-based courses – the proportions are to be determined by the teacher and the learners together if possible, by the teacher alone if necessary.) It is often surprising how much authentic text can be found even in a community where the target language is not the language of general communication. In addition, all kinds of objects ("realia") can be used to make the interactions more realistic, and should be stored away along with the bank of activity types. Games, pictures, and the like, gathered or made by teachers and learners, are also valuable additions to the banks. Addresses of individuals who speak the target language and who might be interested in giving a talk or participating in a project should also be listed – once again, it is surprising how many such people can be located, and how many will generously give their time.

The possibilities are limitless, once the basic framework is in place. The sample materials will illustrate how it is possible to arrive at several different interpretations from one prototypical unit. The use of activities banks ensures that even the same target language unit, once realized, can be used again and again, if the activities are varied by level of difficulty and by content. And the units can be combined into all sorts of "molecular" structures, to provide varied second language courses, each having its own particular design, each responding to the needs of the learners – and of their teachers.

Appendix A Sample task-based frameworks

Framework for units on Monitoring

Objective: 1a
Monitoring the development of a discussion or argument
Focus: Listening
Text types:
Oral: social conversations
meetings
Language skills to be developed:
Recognize: general topic
communicative function or purpose
Deduce meaning and use of lexical items through contextual clues
Recognize: word chains
discourse markers
Project possible outcomes

Appendix A

Objective: 1b
Monitoring to identify the communicative purpose/function
Focus: Listening
Text types:

Oral: conversations
          discussions
          social/social-professional meetings

Language skills to be developed:

Recognize: general topic
                  communicative function or purpose
                  main ideas and supporting arguments
 	
Extract ideas to remember and different lines of thought
 	
Categorize ideas
 	
Infer opinion and attitude
 	
Confirm
Examine
Evaluate   } main points and arguments
Summarize

158

Objective: 1c
Monitoring an interpreter
Focus: Listening
Text types:

Oral: conversations
     discussions
     social/social-professional meetings

Language skills to be developed:

Recognize: general topic
          communicative function or purpose
          details
          use of discourse markers
 	
Extract specific information and ideas to remember
 	
Deduce and infer meaning through contextual clues
 	
Infer opinion and attitude
 	
Examine and confirm: expectations
                        possible outcomes

Objective: 1d

Monitoring for accuracy of content

Focus: Reading

Text types:

Written: correspondence
         translation of reports and correspondence done by secretaries and
         local staff

Language skills to be developed:

Recognize: general topic
          communicative function or purpose
          word chains
          discourse markers

Deduce meaning and use of lexical items through contextual clues

Use: the grammatical system of the target language
     dictionaries

Framework for units on Reading for Information

Objective: 2b
Reading to keep abreast of current events
Focus: Reading/Taking notes
Text types:
Newspaper and local press Local government documents (e.g., bulletins on changes in legislation)
Language skills to be developed:
Find facts Understand facts Recognize fact – distinguish from opinion
Extract main ideas Identify main ideas – distinguish from supporting detail Relate associated ideas
Follow sequence of events
Infer meaning
Follow arguments
Understand/identify cause-and-effect relationships
Make generalizations from content
Summarize and evaluate main points
Summarize and evaluate the implications of the written material

Objective: 2d

Reading in order to "react"/make decisions (e.g., report to/inform Canadian Government and businesses)

Focus: Reading/Taking notes

Text types:
Transactional, written:
newspapers and local press
local government documents (e.g., tender calls, laws, tariff books, statistical data, description of sector and ministries, economic analyses, bulletins interpreting/advising on changes in the law)
street signs/advertisements
official documents pertaining to trade and commerce

Language skills to be developed:

Find and understand facts

Understand: effective details
maps, charts, and tables

Use a variety of sources to determine the reliability of information

Understand technical explanations

Recognize possible options in problematic situations

Analyze and evaluate complex, conflicting ideas and arguments

Draw conclusions

Summarize

Framework for opening and closing encounters in a variety of settings

a.

```
┌─────────▶  Setting: A business meeting in: commercial officer's office
│                                             host's office
│
│
│           Setting: To introduce Canadian business person and/or
├─────────▶          representatives to high-ranking officials in host country,
│                    e.g., at the Canadian Embassy
│
│
├─────────▶  Setting: A social-professional gathering, e.g., in CO's residence
│
│
│           Setting: To initiate/to close the negotiation of a contract, e.g., in
├─────────▶          local authorities' office
│
│
│           Setting: To obtain information outside CO's office, e.g., when
├─────────▶          traveling on business or pleasure outside main centers
│
│
└─────────▶  Student input
```

b. Inventory of speech acts from which to choose

Greet hosts

Introduce self and/or others informally
                                 formally

Make pleasantries

Accept pleasantries

Interpret/understand pleasantries/functions

Identify communicative purpose(s)

Recall previous enounter(s)
        past events

Appendix A

Introduce topic

Understand topic that is being introduced

Reformulate

Paraphrase

Confirm/disagree with information

Discuss follow-up

Predict/announce future related events

Summarize

Express thanks and appreciation

Student input

c. Examples of scenarios to be practiced in the settings outlined in (a)

Note: The scenarios can and will vary according to the target situation.
The scenarios can be coordinated and/or integrated with any one of the scenarios proposed in Frameworks 5, 6, and 7.

Framework 4
Purpose   Scenario 1

I. **Communicative purpose:** Negotiating a contract

II. **Setting:** Local government official's office

Participants: Commercial officer/Canadian business representatives/
Local authorities

Topics: Any topic from the *Directory of Canadian Industry*

Channel: Face-to-face

III. **Stages of the interaction:**

Greetings

Introduce self and others formally

Identify communicative purpose

Present information, e.g., follow-up of initial meeting

LOCAL AUTHORITIES COMPLAIN

Confirm/disagree with information

> **Student input**

Discuss follow-up

Express thanks and appreciation

Take leave

Appendix A

Framework 4
Purpose   Scenario 2

I. **Communicative purpose:** Introducing Canadian business
representatives

II. **Setting:** Canadian Embassy

Participants: Commercial officer/Canadian business representatives/
Local authorities

Topics: New product

Channel: Face-to-face

III. **Stages of the interaction:**

Greetings

Introduce self and others formally

Make and accept pleasantries

Student input

Discuss follow-up

Summarize

Take leave

Framework 4
Purpose   Scenario 3

I. Communicative purpose: Closing the negotiation of a contract

---

II. Setting: Local ministry of foreign affairs

    Participants: Commercial officer/Canadian business representatives/
                 High-ranking government officials

    Topics: Sale of Canadian reactor

    Channel: Face-to-face

III. Stages of the interaction:

Greetings

Identify communicative purpose

Student input

Paraphrase

Summarize

Express thanks and appreciation

Pleasantries

Take leave

Appendix B Frameworks for Communications Needs Courses

Getting around[4]

Cultural considerations

What means of transportation are available?
What form of payment is required: token? ticket? exact fare? cash?
Where do you buy fares?
When do buses, etc., run – on what days? between what hours? how frequently?
Are taxis available?
Is bargaining expected or are fares set?
Can taxis be hailed on the street?
Is tipping expected? How much?
Do strangers share taxis with each other if they are heading in the same direction and taxis are scarce?

Objectives

In this situation, learners will need the language to:
a) get information about public transit
b) find out how to get around
c) use public transit
d) deal with taxis

---

4 By Joyce Pagurek and Brigid Fitzgerald; listening activities illustrated by George Chouchani. Copyright 1984 by Centre for Applied Language Studies, Carleton University. Reprinted by permission.

Objective a) Get information about public transit

Transactions   *Useful words/expressions*

Talk about –location

Does the | #73 | stop | here?
| 1st St. bus | | on Main?

Where is the bus stop?
Where do you get (the 73)?

–availability   Is there a bus on (Main St.)?
Does a bus come by here?

–frequency/schedules   How often does (the 73) come?
When does (the 73) run?
What time does (the 73) run until?
How frequently does (the 73) run on
    Sundays/in peak periods?

–price   How much is a ticket (to Main St.)?
How much for an | adult? |
                | a child? |

–ticket purchase   Can you buy tickets on the bus?
Where do you get tickets?

Additional vocabulary
fare zone
token
exact change
every 10 minutes
every hour (on the half hour)
rush hour

Activities: A) Listening

Tourist: Asks if there is a streetcar/
bus on that street.
Resident: Answers in the affirmative.
Tourist: Asks where to get the bus/
streetcar.
Resident: Shows or points to the stop.

Tourist: Asks about frequency and
schedule of a specific bus/
streetcar.
Operator: Gives information.
Tourist: Asks for further detail (e.g.
how late bus runs; whether
bus runs on weekend, etc.).
Operator: Gives information.

Tourist: Asks where to buy tickets.
Operator: Gives information.
Tourist: Asks for prices for adults,
children (students, seniors).
Operator: Gives information.
Tourist: Thanks operator.

Activities: B) Communication

1. Purpose: to practice getting information about public transportation.
Preparation: review prices, time, days of the week.
Materials: 2 copies of the same *information chart* (real or drawn) with different facts omitted. Example:

Bus	Frequency	Days	Periods of day	Price
2	Every 10 min.	Mon–Sat.	8 a.m. to midnight	Adults 80¢ ea., 5 trips for $3.50
3				Children 50¢ ea.
4	Every 1/2 hour	Daily	7 a.m. 7 p.m.	Seniors 5 trips for $2.00
5				Students
etc.				

Bus	Frequency	Days	Periods of day	Price
2				Adults
3	Every hour on the half hour	Daily	8 a.m. to midnight	Children 40¢ ea., 5 trips for $1.50 Under 5 – free
4				Seniors
5	Every 5 min.	Mon.–Fri.	Rush hour only	Students 60¢ ea., 5 trips for $2.50
etc.				

Activity: Information sharing
Learners work in pairs. Each has an incomplete copy of the same chart. Learners complete their own chart by asking their partners for the missing information.

Eating out[5]

Cultural considerations

What kinds of restaurants are there in the target language country?
Are there special procedures in different kinds of restaurants?
What are the procedures on entering a restaurant?
What about { toasts? seating arrangements?
          { tips? complaints? table manners?
How do you get the waiter's attention?

Objectives

In this situation learners will need the language to:
a) make a reservation
b) order food and drink
c) request service
d) express satisfaction/dissatisfaction (regarding food, bill)

5 By Brigid Fitzgerald and Joyce Pagurek; listening activities illustrated by George Chouchani. Copyright 1984 by Centre for Applied Language Studies, Carleton University. Reprinted by permission.

Objective a) *Make a reservation*

Transactions	*Useful Words/Expressions*
State desire to make a reservation (giving number of people, time, day/date, name, etc.)	I'd like to make a reservation/reserve a table for (number of people) at (time) on (day, date, or time of day). My name is _____. Do you take reservations?
Understand questions about name and spelling, number of people, time/day/date	Name? For what time? When? For how many?
Understand statements about possibility/impossibility of reserving, about availability/ unavailability of space at a given time on a given day	I'm sorry. We don't take reservations. There are no tables available at ____ o'clock.
	Additional vocabulary reserved available free earlier/later tonight/tomorrow

Appendix B

Activities: A) Listening

Customer: States desire to make a reservation for (dinner) for a given number of people for a specific day or time of day (e.g. tonight).
Waiter: Asks for what time.
Customer: States time.
Waiter: States there is space available at that time. Asks for name.
Customer: Gives name.
Waiter: Asks for spelling.
Customer: Spells name.

Customer: Asks if the restaurant takes reservations.
Hostess: Apologizes. Says they do not take reservations.

Customer: States desire to make a reservation (mentioning number of people, specific time and date).
Waiter: Apologizes. States unavailability of table/ space at that time. States time at which tables are available.
Customer: Accepts suggested time. Gives name.
Waiter: Confirms name, time and date. Thanks customer.

Activities: B) Communication

1. *Purpose:* to practice making reservations.
   Preparation: review numbers, days, dates, times, spelling of own name.
   Materials: customer calendar of lunch and dinner appointments; restaurant reservation schedule.

e.g. *Customer's appointment calendar*

Monday	Tuesday	Wednesday	Thursday
Mr. & Mrs. Smith Mr. & Mrs. Jones Dinner 7:30	Business Lunch 1:00 p.m. (Fraser, Richardson & Paquette)	National Secretary Week: take Mary & Jane for lunch 1:30	Nancy's/Tom's birthday Take her/him out for dinner 8:00 p.m.

e.g. *Restaurant reservation schedule*

Monday	Tuesday	Wednesday	Thursday
5:00– 5:30– 6:00– 6:30– 7:00– 7:30– 8:00– 8:30–		12:00– 12:30– 1:00– 1:30– 2:00– 2:30– (closed) 5:00– 5:30– 6:00– 6:30–	5:00– 5:30– 6:00– 6:30– 7:00– 7:30– 8:00– 8:30– 9:00–

Activity: Role-play
Learners work in pairs. The customer has the appointment calendar and the waiter has the restaurant reservation schedule.

The customers call the restaurant (four times) to book reservations for each of the appointments listed in their calendars. They give the information regarding number of people, meal, time, day, etc., as required.

The waiter answers the call, checks the restaurant schedule and, according to the information in the schedule, either
a) books the reservation
b) states an alternative time, if the time requested is not available
c) states there are no reservations at the requested time

The learners reverse roles and repeat the activity with another set of calendars and reservations schedules.

Appendix B

At a post office[6]

Cultural considerations

What services are offered by the post office in the target language country? e.g.
  general delivery; postal boxes; sending telegrams; selling of stamps, etc.
What are the locations, hours and days of operation?
What are the different ways of sending mail? e.g. first class; third class; registered,
  etc.
What are the costs of each and differences in service?

Objectives

In this situation learners will need the language to:
a) mail letters and parcels
b) receive mail (through general delivery or post office box)

6 By Brigid Fitzgerald and Joyce Pagurek; listening activities illustrated by George Chouchani. Copyright 1984 by Centre for Applied Language Studies, Carleton University. Reprinted by permission.

Objective a)   Mail letters and parcels

Transactions	*Useful words/expressions*
State need to send mail to a specific destination	I want to | send | this to _____. | mail |
Talk about –services	How do you want to send it? Surface or air mail? How can I send it? Can I insure it?
–cost of each service	How much is it first class? It's $ _____.
–length of time required	How long will it take (surface mail)? (10) days. Which way is fastest?
Make a purchase	I'll send it air mail. Two aerograms, please. Three 30¢ stamps, please.
Understand instructions	You have to | wrap / tie / seal | the parcel.
Understand refusals	We can't send it. It's too big/heavy, etc.

Additional vocabulary

1st/2nd/3rd class	air letter
air mail	a set of stamps
express	special delivery
insure	new issue
register	faster
wrap, seal, tie	slower, cheapest

Appendix B

Activities: A) Listening

Customer: Asks for specific items (3 aerograms).
Clerk: Supplies these and states price.
Customer: Pays and thanks clerk.

Customer: States destination of parcel and asks about ways to send it.
Clerk: Gives ways and prices.
Customer: Asks about length of time for each.
Clerk: Gives information.
Customer: Selects the way (I'll send it. . .)

Customer: States desire to send a letter using a specific service (e.g. registered mail)
Clerk: States cost.
Customer: Accepts and pays.

Customer: Asks for stamps for a large parcel.
Clerk: Refuses and explains (parcel is not well-wrapped or too big).

Activities: B) Communication

1. *Purpose:* to practice getting and understanding information about sending mail.

   Preparation: review prices, length of time (4 days), names of cities in target language country.

   Materials: copies of the same *postal services* and *rates* charts; in each pair of charts different information is omitted. (If possible, use real charts from post office.) Example:

	Postal Services and Rates					
	Within the Country			Outside the Country		
	1–5 gms.	5–10 gms.	Length of time	1–5 gms.	Over 5 gms.	Length of time
1st class	32¢	5¢ per gm.	3–5 days			
2nd class	25¢	5¢ per gm.	7 days			
3rd class	15¢	4¢ per gm.	10 days			
Air Mail	32¢–64¢	20¢ per gm.	2 days			
Special delivery	add $1.50		Delivery same day as arrival			
Insurance	$2.00					
Registration	$2.00					
etc.						

Note: Omissions can be arranged differently – e.g. each chart has some omissions in both "Within the Country" and "Outside the Country" sections.

Activity: Information sharing

Learners work in pairs. Each has an incomplete copy of the postal services and rates. By asking each other questions they find out the information missing from their charts and fill it in.

Preliminaries: expressing basic concepts
(Time, days, months, dates, seasons, money, location, direction)[7]

Cultural considerations

How do people talk about time in the target language?
  12-hour clock? 24-hour clock?
Is it important for things to happen "on time"?
What does "on time" mean in the target language culture?
When invitations specify a time, how exact is the time?
Is it ever permissible to be late or early for some event?
When does the *afternoon* end and the *evening* begin?
Is there a distinction made between *evening* and *night?*

What is the monetary system in the target language country?
  (e.g. $1.00 = 4 quarters/20 nickels/10 dimes/100 pennies or cents)
Are there colloquial terms for coins, etc.?
When is it important to have change? (e.g. for the bus, the telephone, etc.)

If you need to find your way round in the target language country, who can you ask?

Objectives

To express these concepts learners will need the language to:
a) ask for and give the time
b) talk about days, months, dates, seasons
c) ask about prices
d) ask for and describe interior locations
e) ask for and describe exterior locations
f) ask for and give directions – interior and exterior

---

7 By Joyce Pagurek and Brigid Fitzgerald; listening activities illustrated by George
  Chouchani. Copyright 1984 by Centre for Applied Language Studies, Carleton University. Reprinted by permission.

Objective a) *Ask for and give the time*

Transactions	Useful words/expressions
Ask and give the time	What time is it? Do you have the time? It's ____ o'clock
Ask about and give the time of an engagement	What time/When is the (party)? At ____ o'clock
Ask about and give the time | an event starts/ends | an institution opens/closes |	When does (the game) start/end?

When	does the is	(bank)	open? closed?

etc.

Additional vocabulary

Time expressions: o'clock, thirty, half-past, (twenty) to, (twenty) after, A.M., P.M.

Periods of time/time of day: noon, (at) midnight, (in the) afternoon, (in the) morning, (in the) evening

Institutions: museum, embassy, library, school, etc.

Business: e.g. store, cleaners, drug store, restaurant, office

Engagements: meeting, party, concert, exhibition, class, etc.

Events: movie, games, etc.

Activities: A) Listening

Speaker 1: Asks the time.
Speaker 2: Gives the time.

Speaker 1: Asks about the starting of an event.
Speaker 2: Gives the time.

Speaker 1: Asks about the time of an engagement (e.g. what time is the meeting?)
Speaker 2: Gives the time.

Activities: B) Communication

1. *Purpose:* to practice asking and giving the time.
   Materials: teaching clock or watch.
   Activity: information gathering.
   Learners work in pairs or with the teacher. Learner A asks the time and
   turns the clock/watch to the time Learner B gives. Learner B checks that the
   clock is set at the time which was given. The activity is repeated, using a
   different time for each round. The learners A and B reverse roles.
2. *Purpose:* to practice asking and answering questions about the time of an
   engagement.
   Materials: different sets of *diary cue cards* A & B:

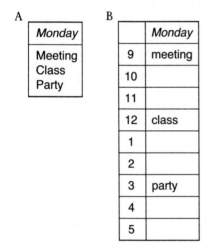

Activity: Information gathering
Learners work in pairs. One learner takes card A, one takes card B.
Learner A begins.
Learner A asks about the time of each engagement on card A.
Learner B answers from the information on card B.
Learner A writes down the times given and checks his answers with Learner B.
The activity is repeated with another set of cards. The learner who has card A
now takes card B.

Preliminaries: Coping[8]

Cultural considerations

How do target language speakers view attempts to speak their language by fluent non-native speakers? by beginners?

How do target language speakers help non-speakers to understand? (e.g. by talking more loudly and deliberately, like English speakers?)

Is it permissible to approach a stranger to request assistance? Who should you *not* approach?

How do target language speakers react to requests for assistance? (e.g., Do they accompany the non-speakers to where they want to go?)

Objectives

At this stage learners will need the language to:

a) make target language speakers aware of the learner's level of ability in the target language.

b) request assistance from target language speakers.

---

8 By Joyce Pagurek and Brigid Fitzgerald; listening activities illustrated by George Chouchani. Copyright 1984 by Centre for Applied Language Studies, Carleton University. Reprinted by permission.

Objective a) Make target language speakers aware of learner's level of ability

Transactions	Useful words/expressions
State inability to speak/understand the target language	I'm sorry, I don't speak _____ I don't understand.
Ask a speaker to speak more slowly	Could you speak slowly, please?
Ask a speaker to repeat what was said	Could you repeat that, please?
Understand an offer to get someone who speaks English	I'll get someone who speaks English.
Ask if anyone speaks English	Is there someone who speaks English?

Activities: A) Listening

Teacher: States the hours of the class.
Student: Asks for repetition.
Teacher: States class hours again – slowly.

Clerk: Asks (learner's name).
Learner: Apologizes; says he doesn't understand. Asks if there is someone who speaks English.
Clerk: Says yes.

Passerby: Asks learner a question.
Learner: Says she doesn't speak the language.
Passerby: Apologizes.

Activities: B) Communication

1. *Purpose*: to practice (a) saying that one doesn't understand, or that one doesn't speak the language, and (b) asking the speaker to repeat or speak more slowly.

Activity:
The teacher speaks to the class in the target language (e.g. about timetable, office hours, etc.). Learners who do not understand at all indicate this by using expressions from (a). Learners who think they understand but would like to hear the information again or more slowly indicate this by using expressions from (b). If necessary, the teacher conveys the information in another way (e.g. by translating, by drawing on the board, miming, etc.).

Preliminaries: First steps toward communications[9]

Cultural considerations

Are people formal/informal when they address/introduce people?
What body language should you be aware of (e.g. shaking hands – is this appropriate/acceptable?)
Do people stand close to/far from each other when speaking?
What topics are considered acceptable/taboo when first meeting people? (e.g. religion, marital status, etc.)

Objectives

In this situation, learners will need the language to:
a) make introductions (self and others)
   –state origin/nationality
   –use correct forms of address
b) greet and take leave
c) give personal information: name
d) give personal information: phone number, address
e) give further personal information: religion, occupation, marital/family status

9 By Joyce Pagurek and Brigid Fitzgerald; listening activities illustrated by George Chouchani. Copyright 1984 by Centre for Applied Language Studies, Carleton University. Reprinted by permission.

Objective a)   Make introductions

Transactions	*Useful words/expressions*
Introduce oneself and say where one is from/one's nationality	I'm (name). My name is _____. I'd like to introduce myself. I don't think we've met. (etc.) I come from | I'm from |(country) I'm (nationality).
Understand questions about origins/ nationality	Where are you from? Are you (nationality)?
Respond to introductions	Hello./How do you do. Nice to meet you. (etc.)
Introduce equals and superiors and address people correctly	Mr./Mrs./Miss/Ms./ (last name) Doctor/Professor/Rabbi/Reverend/Father/ Officer/Judge/etc. I'd like you to meet _____. This is _____. May I introduce _____. Have you met _____? etc.

Additional vocabulary

(my) son	father
daughter	boss
husband	friend
wife	teacher etc.
mother	
please	thanks
thank you	I'm sorry

Activities: A) Listening

Student 1: Introduces self and states where he is from.
Student 2: Introduces self (to student 1) and states where she is from.

Tom: Introduces his friends, Bob and Mary.
Mary: Greets Bob.
Bob: Greets Mary.

Student: Introduces his professor (Professor Smith) to his mother (Mrs. Evans).
Professor Smith: Greets the mother.
Mrs. Evans: Greets professor.

Boss: Introduces new employee to another employee.
Employees: Greet each other.
Boss: Introduces new employee and the manager.
Partner: Greets new employee.
New employee: Greets partner.

Activities: B) Communication

1. *Purpose:* to practice introducing oneself and saying where one is from.
   Activity: Role-play: Learners circulate and introduce themselves to the others
   in the class by giving their names and saying where they are from:
   A: I'm A. I'm from (Canada).
   B: (Hello) I'm B. I'm from (Brazil).
2. *Purpose:* to practice introducing others using correct form(s) of address.
   Materials: situations list:

---

1. You are with your mother – you meet your friend
2. You are with your friend – you meet another friend
3. You are with your friend – you meet your professor
4. You are with your spouse – you meet your boss
5. You are with your friend – you meet your grandfather
6. You are with your son/daughter – you meet a co-worker, etc.

Activity: Role-play
Learners form groups of three. Each learner selects (or is given) one or more
situations from the situations list.

For each situation, one learner does the introducing and the other two learners take the roles of the strangers to be introduced. The "strangers" respond
appropriately to the introductions. (Learners should invent names for the
strangers.)

References

Agar, M. 1980. *The Professional Stranger: An Informal Introduction to Ethnography*. London: Academic Press.

Agard, F. 1968. *Modern Approach to Spanish*. Rev. ed. Teacher's Manual. New York: Holt, Reinhart and Winston.

Akinnaso, F., and C. Ajirotutu. 1982. "Performance and ethnic style in job interviews." In Gumperz, ed. (1982), pp. 119–44.

Alatis, J. E. (ed.). 1978. *International Dimensions of Bilingualism*. Georgetown Round Table on Languages and Linguistics. Washington, D.C.: Georgetown University Press.

Alatis, J. E., H. B. Altman, and P. M. Alatis (eds.). 1981. *The Second Language Classroom: Direction for the 1980's*. Oxford: Oxford University Press.

Alexander, L. 1975. "Some methodological implications of *Waystage* and *Threshold Level*." In van Ek (1980), pp. 235–51; and in van Ek, Alexander, and Kirkpatrick (1980), pp. 85–101.

Allen, J. P. B. 1980. "A three-level curriculum model for second language education." Keynote address at the Annual Conference of the Ontario Modern Language Teachers' Association. Mimeo: Modern Language Centre, Ontario Institute for Studies in Education.

1984. "General-purpose language teaching: a variable focus approach." In Brumfit, ed. (1984c), pp. 61–74.

Allen, J. P. B., and H. G. Widdowson. 1974a. "Teaching the communicative use of English." *IRAL* 12: 1–21.

1974b. *English in Focus* series. London: Oxford University Press.

Allwright, R. 1979. "Language learning through communication practice." In Brumfit and Johnson, eds. (1979), pp. 167–82.

Altman, H., and C. James (eds.). 1980. *Foreign Language Teaching: Meeting Individual Needs*. Oxford: Pergamon Press.

Asher, J. J. 1977. *Learning Another Language Through Actions: The Complete Teacher's Guidebook*. Los Gatos, Cal.: Sky Oaks Productions.

Austin, J. L. 1962. *How to Do Things with Words*. Cambridge, Mass.: Harvard University Press.

Bachman, L., and A. Palmer. 1982. "The construct validation of some components of communicative proficiency." *TESOL Quarterly* 16/4: 449–64.

Bell, R. 1982. "The language problems of the European Community: some suggestions derived from a general theory of language and educational planning." In van Deth and Puyo, eds. (1982), pp. 255–8.

Beretta, A., and A. Davies. 1985. "Evaluation of the Bangalore project." *ELT Journal* 39: 121–7.

Bialystok, E. 1983. "Some factors in the selection and implementation of communication strategies." In Faerch and Kasper, eds., pp. 100–18.

References

Bibeau, G. 1982. *L'Education bilingue en Amérique du Nord*. Montréal: Guérin.
  1983. "La théorie du Moniteur de Krashen: aspects critiques." *Bulletin de l'association canadienne de linguistique appliquée* 5/1: 99–123.
Bolinger, D., J. Ciruti, and H. Montero (eds.). 1966. *Modern Spanish*. 2nd ed. New York: Harcourt, Brace and World.
Breen, M. P. 1984. "Process syllabuses for the language classroom." In Brumfit, ed. (1984c), pp. 47–60.
Breen, M. P., and C. N. Candlin. 1980. "The essentials of a communicative curriculum in language teaching." *Applied Linguistics* 1: 89–221.
Breen, M., C. Candlin, and A. Waters. 1979. "Communicative materials design: some basic principles." *RELC Journal* 10: 1–13.
Brown, G., and G. Yule. 1983. *Discourse Analysis*. Cambridge: Cambridge University Press.
Brown, H. (ed.). 1976. *Papers in Second Language Acquisition*. Ann Arbor, Mich.: Language Learning.
  1980. "The role of teacher feedback in preventing the fossilized errors of second language learners." *Contact* 7: 5–7.
Brumfit, C. 1980. "From defining to designing: communicative specifications versus communicative methodology in foreign-language teaching." In Müller, ed. (1980), pp. 1–9.
  1981. "Notional syllabuses revisited: a response." *Applied Linguistics* 2: 90–2.
  1982. "Methodological solutions to the problem of communicative competence." In Hines and Rutherford, eds. (1982), pp. 71–8.
  1984a. "The Bangalore procedural syllabus." *ELT Journal* 34: 233–41.
  1984b. *Communicative Methodology in Language Teaching: The Roles of Fluency and Accuracy*. Cambridge: Cambridge University Press.
  (ed.). 1984c. *General English Syllabus Design: Curriculum and Syllabus Design for the General English Classroom*. ELT Documents 118. Oxford: British Council and Pergamon Press.
Brumfit, C. J., and K. Johnson (eds.). 1979. *The Communicative Approach to Language Teaching*. London: Oxford University Press.
Canadian Committee on Modern Languages. 1928. *Modern Language Instruction in Canada*. Vol. 1. Toronto: University of Toronto Press.
Canale, M. 1983. "From communicative competence to communicative language pedagogy." In Richards and Schmidt, eds. (1983), pp. 2–27.
Canale, M., and M. Swain. 1980. "Theoretical bases of communicative approaches to second-language teaching and testing." *Applied Linguistics* 1: 1–47.
Candlin, C. 1973. "The status of pedagogical grammars." In Corder and Roulet, eds. (1973), pp. 55–64.
  1976. "Communicative language teaching and the debt to pragmatics." In Rameh, ed. (1976), pp. 237–56.
  (ed.). 1981. *The Communicative Teaching of English: Principles and an Exercise Typology*. London: Longman.
  1984. "Syllabus design as a critical process." In Brumfit, ed. (1984c), pp. 29–46.
Candlin, C. N., and M. P. Breen. 1979. "Evaluating and designing language

teaching materials." *Practical Papers in English Language Education* 2: 172–216.

Carroll, B. 1980. *Testing Communicative Performance: An Interim Study.* Oxford: Pergamon Press.

Carroll, J. 1953. *The Study of Language.* Cambridge, Mass.: Harvard University Press.

Chomsky, N. 1965. *Aspects of the Theory of Syntax.* Cambridge, Mass.: MIT Press.

1966. "Linguistic theory." In Mead, ed. (1966), pp. 43–9.

Cole, P., and T. Morgan (eds.). 1975. *Syntax and Semantics.* Vol. 3: *Speech Acts.* New York: Academic Press.

Corder, S. P. 1973. *Introducing Applied Linguistics.* Harmondsworth: Penguin.

1978. "Trends in EFL." *SPEAQ Journal* 2: 11–23.

Corder, S. P., and E. Roulet (eds.). 1973. *Theoretical Linguistic Models in Applied Linguistics.* Brussels: AIMAV.

Coste, D., J. Courtillon, V. Ferenczi, M. Martins-Baltar, E. Papo, and E. Roulet. 1976. *Un niveau seuil.* Strasbourg: Council of Europe.

Coulthard, J. 1977. *An Introduction to Discourse Analysis.* London: Longman.

CREDIF. 1962. *Voix et images de France.* Paris: Didier.

Crombie, W. 1985. *Process and Relation in Discourse and Language Learning.* Oxford: Oxford University Press.

Cumming, A. 1984. "Simulation or reality? A group project in writing." *Carleton Papers in Applied Language Studies* 1: 147–58.

Davies, A., C. Criper, and A. Howatt (eds.). 1984. *Interlanguage.* Edinburgh: Edinburgh University Press.

Deighton, L. C. (ed.). 1971. *Encyclopedia of Education.* New York: Macmillan.

Ellis, R. 1981. "The role of input in language acquisition: some implications for second language teaching." *Applied Linguistics* 2: 70–82.

1984. *Classroom Second Language Development.* Oxford: Pergamon Press.

Faerch, C., and G. Kasper (eds.). 1983. *Strategies in Interlanguage Communication.* London: Longman.

Faerch, C., K. Haastrup, and R. Phillipson. 1984. *Learner Language and Language Learning.* Copenhagen: Gyldendals Sprogbibliotek.

Firth, J. R. 1968. *Selected Papers: 1952–59.* Edited by F. R. Palmer. London: Longman.

Fitzgerald, B., and J. Pagurek. 1984a. *Teachers' Handbook for the Frameworks for Communication Needs Courses, Survival and General Purposes.* Ottawa: Centre for Applied Language Studies, Carleton University.

1984b. *Frameworks for Communication Needs Courses: First Steps Towards Communication, Expressing Basic Concepts, Coping, Getting Around, Eating Out, At a Post Office.* Ottawa: Centre for Applied Language Studies, Carleton University.

Fraser, B. 1978. "Acquiring social competence in a second language." *RELC Journal* 9: 1–21.

Fraser, W. A., and J. Squair. 1900. *French Grammar and Reader.* Toronto: Copp, Clark Co. Ltd.

Freedman, A., and I. Pringle (eds.). 1980. *Reinventing the Rhetorical Tradition.*

References

Conway, Ark.: L and S Books, University of Central Arkansas, for the Canadian Council of Teachers of English.

Freedman, A., I. Pringle, and J. Yalden (eds.). 1983. *Learning to Write: First Language/Second Language.* London: Longman.

French, Core Programs. 1980. Toronto: Ontario Ministry of Education.

Freudenstein, R., J. Beneke, and H. Pönisch (eds.). 1981. *Language Incorporated: Teaching Foreign Languages in Industry.* Oxford/Munich: Pergamon Press/Max Hueber Verlag.

Fröhlich, M., N. Spada, and P. Allen. 1985. "Differences in the communicative orientation of L2 classrooms." *TESOL Quarterly* 19: 27–58.

Genesee, F. 1983. "Bilingual education of majority-language children: the immersion experiments in review." *Applied Psycholinguistics* 4: 1–46.

Gingras, R. (ed.). 1978. *Second Language Acquisition and Foreign Language Teaching.* Washington, D.C.: Center for Applied Linguistics.

Gouvernement du Québec. 1980. *Programmes d'études, anglais et français langues secondes.* Québec: Ministère de l'éducation, Direction générale du développement pédagogique.

Greenwood, J. 1985. "Bangalore revisited: a reluctant complaint." *ELT Journal* 39: 268–73.

Gregg, K. R. 1984. "Krashen's Monitor and Occam's Razor." *Applied Linguistics* 5: 79–100.

Grellet, F. 1981. *Developing Reading Skills.* Cambridge: Cambridge University Press.

Grice, H. P. 1975. "Logic and conversation." In Cole and Morgan, eds. (1975), pp. 41–58.

Gumperz, J. (ed.). 1982. *Language and Social Identity.* Cambridge: Cambridge University Press.

Gumperz, J., and J. Cook-Gumperz. 1982. "Interethnic communication in committee negotiations." In Gumperz, ed. (1982), pp. 145–62.

Halliday, M. A. K. 1970. "Language structure and language function." In Lyons, ed. (1970), pp. 140–65.

1975. *Learning How to Mean: Explorations in the Development of Language.* London: Edward Arnold.

1978. *Language as a Social Semiotic.* London: Edward Arnold.

Halliday, M. A. K., and R. Hasan. 1976. *Cohesion in English.* London: Longman.

Halliday, M. A. K., A. McIntosh, and P. Strevens. 1964. *The Linguistic Sciences and Language Teaching.* London: Longman.

Hampshire, S. 1968. "Stuart Hampshire and Noam Chomsky discuss the study of language." *The Listener,* Vol. 79, May 30.

Handscombe, J., R. A. Orem, and B. P. Taylor (eds.). 1984. *On TESOL '83: The Question of Control.* Washington, D.C.: Teachers of English to Speakers of Other Languages.

Hartmann, R. R. K., and F. C. Stork. 1972. *Dictionary of Language and Linguistics.* New York: Wiley.

Hills, E., J. Ford, and G. Rivera. 1949. *A Brief Spanish Grammar for Colleges.* Boston: D. C. Heath.

References

Hines, M., and W. Rutherford (eds.). 1982. *On TESOL 1981*. Washington, D.C.: Teachers of English to Speakers of Other Languages.

Høedt, J. 1981. "The study of needs analysis." In Høedt and Turner, eds. (1981), pp. 77–89.

Høedt, J., and R. Turner (eds.). 1981. *New Bearings in LSP*. Copenhagen: The LSP Centre, UNESCO ALSED LSP Network and Newsletter, and the Copenhagen School of Economics.

Høedt, J., et al. (eds.). 1982. *Pragmatics and LSP: Proceedings of the 3rd European Symposium on LSP*. Copenhagen: The LSP Centre, UNESCO ALSED LSP Network and Newsletter, and the Copenhagen School of Economics.

Holec, H. 1980. "Learner needs: meeting needs in self-directed learning." In Altman and James, eds. (1980), pp. 30–45.

1981. *Autonomy and Foreign Language Learning*. Oxford: Pergamon Press. (First published 1979 by the Council of Europe, Strasbourg.)

Hornby, A. S. 1950. "The situational approach in language teaching." A series of three articles in *English Language Teaching* 4: Issues 4–6.

Howatt, A. 1984. *A History of English Language Teaching*. Oxford: Oxford University Press.

Hyltenstam, K., and M. Pienemann (eds.). 1985. *Modelling and Assessing Second Language Acquisition*. Clevedon: Multilingual Matters.

Hymes, D. 1967. "Models of the interaction of language and social setting." *Journal of Social Issues* 23: 8–28.

1972. "On communicative competence." In Pride and Holmes, eds. (1972), pp. 269–93.

Jakobovits, L. 1970. *Foreign Language Learning: A Psycholinguistic Analysis of the Issues*. Rowley, Mass.: Newbury House.

Jakobson, R. 1960. "Closing statement: linguistics and poetics." In Seboek, ed. (1960), pp. 350–77.

James, C. (ed.). 1985. *Foreign Language Proficiency in the Classroom and Beyond*. Lincolnwood: National Textbook Co.

Johnson, K. 1980. " 'Systematic' and 'non-systematic' components in a communicative approach to language teaching." Mimeo: Paper delivered at the Berne Colloquium. Department of Linguistics, Reading University.

1982. *Communicative Syllabus Design and Methodology*. Oxford: Pergamon Press.

Jones, L. 1977. *Functions of English*. Cambridge: Cambridge University Press. (2nd ed. 1981.)

Judd, E. L. 1984. "TESOL as a political act: a moral question." In Handscombe, Orem and Taylor, eds. (1984), pp. 263–72.

Jupp, T. C., and S. Hodlin. 1975. *Industrial English*. London: Heinemann.

Kaplan, R. 1972. *The Anatomy of Rhetoric: Prolegomena to a Functional Theory of Rhetoric*. Philadelphia: Centre for Curriculum Development.

1978. "Contrastive rhetoric: some hypotheses." *ITL* 39–40: 61–72.

(ed.). 1980. *On the Scope of Applied Linguistics*. Rowley, Mass.: Newbury House.

1983. "Contrastive rhetorics: some implications for the writing process." In Freedman, Pringle, and Yalden, eds. (1983), pp. 139–61.

References

Kelly, L. G. 1969. *25 Centuries of Language Teaching.* Rowley, Mass.: Newbury House.
Krashen, S. 1978. "Adult second language acquisition and learning: a review of theory and practice." In Gingras, ed. (1978), pp. 1–26.
   1981. *Second Language Acquisition and Second Language Learning.* Oxford: Pergamon Press.
   1982. *Principles and Practice in Second Language Acquisition.* Oxford: Pergamon Press.
Krashen, S., and T. Terrell. 1983. *The Natural Approach: Language Acquisition in the Classroom.* Oxford: Alemany Press/Pergamon Press.
Kress, G. (ed.). 1976. *Halliday: System and Function in Language.* London: Oxford University Press.
Lackstrom, J., L. Selinker, and L. Trimble. 1973. "Technical rhetorical principles and grammatical choice." *TESOL Quarterly* 7: 127–36.
Lado, R. 1970. *Lado English Series.* Montréal: Centre Educatif et Culturel.
Lado, R., and E. Blansitt. 1967. *Manual for Instructors and Teaching Assistants to Accompany Contemporary Spanish.* New York: McGraw-Hill.
Lado, R., and C. C. Fries. 1958. *English Pattern Practices.* Ann Arbor: University of Michigan Press.
Larsen-Freeman, D. (ed.). 1980. *Discourse Analysis in Second Language Research.* Rowley, Mass.: Newbury House.
   1982. "The 'what' of second language acquisition." In Hines and Rutherford, eds. (1982), pp. 107–28.
Lightbown, P. M. 1984. "The relationship between theory and method in second language acquisition research." In Davies, Criper, and Howatt, eds. (1984), pp. 241–52.
   1985. "Great expectations: second-language acquisition research and classroom teaching." *Applied Linguistics* 6: 173–89.
Littlewood, W. 1981. *Communicative Language Teaching: An Introduction.* Cambridge: Cambridge University Press.
Long, M. 1983a. "Does second language instruction make a difference? A review of research." *TESOL Quarterly* 17: 359–82.
   1983b. "Role: an unresolved dimension in language learning." *RELC Journal* 14/2: 54–9.
   1985. "A role for instruction in second language acquisition: task-based language training." In Hyltenstam and Pienemann, eds. (1985), pp. 77–100.
Long, M., and P. Porter. 1985. "Group work, interlanguage talk, and second language acquisition." *TESOL Quarterly* 19: 207–28.
Long, M., and C. Sato. 1984. "Methodological issues in interlanguage studies: an interactionist perspective." In Davies, Criper, and Howatt, eds. (1984), pp. 253–79.
Lyons, J. (ed.). 1970. *New Horizons in Linguistics.* Harmondsworth: Penguin.
Mackay, R. 1978. "Identifying the nature of the learner's needs." In Mackay and Mountford, eds. (1978), pp. 21–42.
Mackay, R., and M. Bosquet. 1981. "LSP curriculum development – from policy to practice." In Mackay and Palmer, eds. (1981), pp. 1–28.
Mackay, R., and A. Mountford (eds.). 1978. *English for Specific Purposes: A Case Study Approach.* London: Longman.

Mackay, R., and J. Palmer (eds.). 1981. *Languages for Specific Purposes*. Rowley, Mass.: Newbury House.

Mackey, W. F. 1965. *Language Teaching Analysis*. London: Longman.

Malinowski, B. 1923. "The problem of meaning in primitive languages." Reprinted in Ogden and Richards, eds. (1946), pp. 296–336.

McGroarty, M. 1984. "Some meanings of communicative competence for second language students." *TESOL Quarterly* 18: 257–72.

Mead, R. G. (ed.). 1966. *Language Teaching: Broader Contexts*. Northeast Conference on the Teaching of Foreign Languages: Reports of the Working Committees. New York: MLA Materials Center.

Meisel, J. M., H. Clahsen, and M. Pienemann. 1981. "On determining developmental stages in natural language acquisition." *Studies in Second Language Acquisition* 3: 109–35.

Mollica, A., and J. Yalden. 1984. *English and French as Second Languages in Canadian Teacher-Education Institutions*. Welland, Ontario: Canadian Modern Language Review/Revue canadienne des langues vivantes.

Müller, K. E. (ed.). 1980. *The Foreign Language Syllabus and Communicative Approaches to Teaching: Proceedings of a European-American Seminar*. Special issue of *Studies in Second Language Acquisition* 3/1.

Munby, J. 1978. *Communicative Syllabus Design*. Cambridge: Cambridge University Press.

Naiman, N., M. Fröhlich, H. H. Stern, and A. Todesco. 1978. *The Good Language Learner*. Toronto: Ontario Institute for Studies in Education.

Ogden, C. K., and I. A. Richards. 1946. *The Meaning of Meaning*. 8th ed. London: Routledge and Kegan Paul.

Osgood, C. E., and Sebeok, T. A. (eds.). 1954. "Psycholinguistics: a survey of theory and research problems." *Journal of Abnormal and Social Psychology* 49: Supplement. Reprinted as *Psycholinguistics: A Survey of Theory and Research Problems* along with *A Survey of Psycholinguistic Research, 1954–1964* by A. R. Diebold. Bloomington: Indiana University Press, 1965.

Pienemann, M. 1984. "Psychological constraints on the teachability of languages." *Studies in Second Language Acquisition* 6: 186–214.

Politzer, R. L., and M. McGroarty. 1985. "An exploratory study of learning behaviors and their relationship to gains in linguistic and communicative competence." *TESOL Quarterly* 19: 103–24.

Pride, J. B., and J. Holmes (eds.). 1972. *Sociolinguistics*. Harmondsworth: Penguin.

Rameh, C. (ed.). 1976. *Semantics: Theory and Application*. Georgetown University Round Table on Languages and Linguistics. Washington, D.C.: Georgetown University Press.

Richards, J. C., and T. Rodgers. 1982. "Method: approach, design, and procedure." *TESOL Quarterly* 16: 153–68.

Richards, J. C., and R. W. Schmidt (eds.). 1983. *Language and Communication*. London: Longman.

Richterich, R., and Chancerel, J.-L. 1980. *Identifying the Needs of Adults Learning a Foreign Language*. Oxford: Pergamon Press. (First published 1977 by the Council of Europe, Strasbourg.)

Richterich, R., et al. 1981. "Préoccupations actuelles des chercheurs européens

References

en didactique des langues." Actes du 12e colloque annuel. *Bulletin de l'Acla,* Automne: 195–207.

Riley, P. (ed.). 1985. *Discourse and Learning: Papers in Applied Linguistics and Language Learning from the C.R.A.P.E.L.* London: Longman.

Ritchie, R. 1955. *A Junior Manual of French Composition.* Cambridge: Cambridge University Press.

Robertson, A. S. 1971. "Curriculum building." In Deighton, ed. (1971), pp. 564–75.

Robinson, P. 1980. *ESP (English for Specific Purposes).* Oxford: Pergamon Press.

Roulet, E. 1972. *Théories grammaticales, descriptions et enseignement des langues.* Paris/Bruxelles: Fernand Nathan/Labor.

Rubin, J., and I. Thompson. 1982. *How to Be a More Successful Language Learner.* Boston: Heinle and Heinle.

Savignon, S. 1972. *Communicative Competence: An Experiment in Foreign Language Teaching.* Philadelphia: Center for Curriculum Development.

1983. *Communicative Competence: Theory and Classroom Practice.* Reading, Mass.: Addison-Wesley.

1985. "Evaluation of communicative competence: the ACTFL provisional proficiency guidelines." *Modern Language Journal* 69: 129–42.

Scherer, G., and Wertheimer, M. 1964. *A Psycholinguistic Experiment in Foreign-Language Teaching.* New York: McGraw-Hill.

Schutz, N., and B. Derwing. 1981. "The problem of needs assessment in English for Specific Purposes: some theoretical and practical considerations." In Mackay and Palmer, eds. (1981), pp. 29–44.

Searle, J. R. 1969. *Speech Acts: An Essay in the Philosophy of Language.* Cambridge: Cambridge University Press.

Seboek, T. (ed.). 1960. *Style in Language.* Cambridge, Mass.: MIT Press.

Selinker, L. 1984. "The current state of IL studies: an attempted critical summary." In Davies, Criper, and Howatt, eds. (1984), pp. 332–43.

Selinker, L., and L. Trimble. 1974. "Formal written communication and ESL." *Journal of Technical Writing and Communication* 4: 81–91.

Selinker, L., E. Tarone, and V. Hanzeli (eds.). 1981. *English for Academic and Technical Purposes.* Rowley, Mass.: Newbury House.

Selinker, L., R. M. Todd Trimble, and L. Trimble. 1978. "Rhetorical function-shifts in EST discourse." *TESOL Quarterly* 12: 311–20.

Sharwood-Smith, M. 1981. "Consciousness-raising and the second language learner." *Applied Linguistics* 2: 159–69.

Shaw, P. A. 1982. "Ad hoc needs analysis." *Modern English Teacher* 9/2: 12–14.

Skinner, B. 1957. *Verbal Behavior.* New York: Appleton-Century-Crofts.

Smith, P. D. 1970. *A Comparison of the Cognitive and Audiolingual Approaches to Foreign Language Instruction: The Pennsylvania Foreign Language Project.* Philadelphia: Center for Curriculum Development.

1971. *Toward a Practical Theory of Second Language Instruction.* Philadelphia: Center for Curriculum Development.

Spolsky, B. 1978. *Educational Linguistics: An Introduction.* Rowley, Mass.: Newbury House.

Stern, H. H. 1980. "Some approaches to communicative language teaching in Canada." In Müller, ed. (1980), pp. 57–63.

1981. "Communicative language teaching and learning: toward a synthesis." In Alatis, Altman, and Alatis, eds. (1981), pp. 131–48.

1983. *Fundamental Concepts of Language Teaching.* Oxford: Oxford University Press.

Strevens, P. 1977. *New Orientations in the Teaching of English.* Oxford: Oxford University Press.

1985a. "Patterns in the organization of teacher training." In K. Jankowsky (ed.), *Scientific and Humanistic Dimensions of Language: Festschrift for Robert Lado,* pp. 95–104. Amsterdam: John Benjamins Publishing Co.

1985b. "Language learning and language teaching: towards an integrated model." LSA/TESOL Institute 1985: Forum Lecture. Mimeo. The Bell Educational Trust, Cambridge.

Stubbs, M. 1983. *Discourse Analysis: The Sociolinguistic Analysis of Natural Language.* Oxford: Blackwell.

Swain, M. 1978. "Bilingual education for the English-speaking Canadian." In Alatis, ed. (1978), pp. 141–54.

1981. "Bilingual education for majority and minority language children." *Studia Linguistica* 35: 15–23.

Tarone, E. 1983. "On the variability of interlanguage systems." *Applied Linguistics* 4: 142–63.

Tarone, E., U. Frauenfelder, and L. Selinker. 1976. "Systematicity/variability and stability/instability in interlanguage systems." In Brown, ed. (1976), pp. 93–134.

Terrell, T. 1977. "A natural approach to second language acquisition and learning." *Modern Language Journal* 61: 325–37.

1982. "The Natural Approach to language teaching: an update." *Modern Language Journal* 66: 121–32.

Thomas, J. 1983. "Cross-cultural pragmatic failure." *Applied Linguistics* 4: 91–112.

Titone, R. 1968. *Teaching Foreign Languages: An Historical Sketch.* Washington, D.C.: Georgetown University Press.

Todd Trimble, M., and L. Trimble. 1982. "Rhetorical-grammatical features of scientific and technical texts as a major factor in written ESP communication." In Høedt et al., eds. (1982), pp. 199–216.

Trim, J. L. M. 1980. "Draft outline of a European unit/credit system for modern language learning by adults." In Trim et al., eds. (1980), pp. 15–28.

Trim, J. L. M., R. Richterich, J. A. van Ek, and D. A. Wilkins. 1980. *Systems Development in Adult Language Learning: A European Unit/Credit System for Modern Language Learning by Adults.* Oxford: Pergamon Press. (First published 1973 by the Council of Europe, Strasbourg.)

Ullmann, R. 1982. "A broadened curriculum framework for second languages." *ELT Journal* 36: 255–62.

van Deth, J.-P., and J. Puyo (eds.). 1982. *Statut et gestion des langues.* Actes du 2e colloque international "Langues et coopération européene." Paris: CIREEL.

References

van Ek, J. 1980. "The threshold level in a unit/credit system." In Trim et al., eds. (1980), pp. 89–146.

1976. *The Threshold Level for Modern Language Learning in Schools*. London: Longman.

1980. *Threshold Level English*. Oxford: Pergamon Press. (First published 1975 by the Council of Europe, Strasbourg.)

van Ek, J., L. Alexander, and M. Kirkpatrick. 1980. *Waystage*. Oxford: Pergamon, Press. (First published 1977 by the Council of Europe, Strasbourg.)

Wesche, M. 1985. "Immersion and the universities." *Canadian Modern Language Review/Revue canadienne des langues vivantes* 41: 931–40.

Widdowson, H. G. 1978. *Teaching Language as Communication*. Oxford: Oxford University Press.

(ed.). 1979. *Discovering Discourse: Reading and Thinking in English*. Oxford: Oxford University Press.

1983. *Learning Purpose and Language Use*. Oxford: Oxford University Press.

1984. "Educational and pedagogic factors in syllabus design." In Brumfit, ed. (1984c), pp. 23–8.

Wilkins, D. A. 1976. *Notional Syllabuses*. London: Oxford University Press.

1981. "Notional syllabuses revisited." *Applied Linguistics* 2: 83–9.

Wolfson, N. 1983. "Rules of speaking." In Richards and Schmidt, eds. (1983), pp. 61–88.

Yalden, J. 1983. *The Communicative Syllabus: Evolution, Design and Implementation*. Oxford: Pergamon Press.

1984. "The design process in communicative language teaching." *Canadian Modern Language Review/Revue canadienne des langues vivantes* 40: 398–413.

Yalden, J., and M. Bosquet. 1984a. "Analysis and description of communication needs and design of prototypes for the preparation of language specific pedagogic materials." Report prepared for the Department of External Affairs, Government of Canada. Centre for Applied Language Studies, Carleton University, Ottawa.

1984b. "Frameworks for communication needs courses, intermediate level." Report prepared for the Department of External Affairs, Government of Canada. Centre for Applied Language Studies, Carleton University, Ottawa.

Yalden, J., and C. S. Jones. 1984. *Communication Needs Course in Bahasa Indonesia*. Carleton University, Ottawa: Centre for Applied Language Studies.

Young, L., and B. Fitzgerald. 1982. *Listening and Learning Lectures*. Rowley, Mass.: Newbury House.

Index

accountability, 85
activities banks, 129, 153–6
Agard, F., 55
applied linguistics, 7, 18, 36
Army Method, 63
Asher, J., 71
Austin, J. L., 35
authentic text, 156

Bachman, L., 22
Bahasa Indonesia, *see* frameworks, discourse-based
Bangalore project, 65–6, 67
basic bookshelf, 154
behaviorism, 51, 53–4
Bell, R., 60
Breen, M., 125
Brumfit, C. J., 9, 10, 23, 61, 76, 88 fn., 90

Canale, M., 19–21
Candlin, C., 47, 75, 76, 125
Chomsky, N., 15–18, 33, 60
classroom techniques, 71
  see also communicative activities
communication, 19, 20
Communication Needs Courses (CNCs), 105, 112, 118, 121, 126, 140
communication strategies, 44
communicative activities, 105, 106, 118, 151–2
  see also learning activities; tasks
communicative approach, *see* communicative language teaching
communicative competence, 16, 21, 23, 25, 31, 48, 60, 84, 94, 96

and "capacity," 42
components of, 19–24, 42, 84, 88, 90
discourse, 20–2, 88, 96
fluency, 22, 23
as a goal, 25–6
grammatical/linguistic, 19, 20–2, 24, 26, 88, 95, 96
interactional patterns, 22
lexis, 22
and performance, 20, 96
phonology/orthography, 22
pragmatic, 22
propositional content, 22
sociolinguistic, 20–2, 88, 96
strategic, 20–2, 95
  see also language use
communicative interaction, 47, 57
communicative language teaching, 51, 57, 61, 74, 151
grammar in, 152–3
models of, 61–6
naturalistic versions of, 73
process-oriented, 74
communicative methodology, 62
communicative proficiency, *see* proficiency
competence and performance, 20
  see also Chomsky, N.
contrastive analysis, 4
contrastive rhetoric, 46
conversational analysis, 44
cooperative principle, 42–3
Corder, S. P., 60
Coulthard, J., 44
Council of Europe, 30, 60
course content, 93, 113
course design, 3–6, 19, 25, 26, 29, 68, 69, 74, 85, 92, 94, 130, 148

203